Disc

MW00888311

Contents

Your feedback is invaluable to us

If you recently bought this book, we would love to hear from you!

You can do this by writing a review on Amazon (or the online store where you purchased this book) about your last purchase! As part of our continual service improvement process, we love to hear real client experiences and feedback.

How does it work?

To post a review on Amazon, just log in to your account and click on the Create Your Own Review button (under Customer Reviews) of the relevant product page. You can find examples of product reviews in Amazon. If you purchased from another online store, simply follow their procedures.

Medical director

Medical director 2573 calculating self Assessment & Interview Preparation Questions:

Follow-up and Control

1. How do you get Medical director sensitive data for current performance other reviews?

2. How do you evaluate the productivity/effectiveness of your subordinates?

3. How do you keep track of what your subordinates are doing?

4. What administrative paperwork do you have? Is it useful? Why/why not?

5. How did you keep track of delegated assignments?

Ambition

1. Is ambition inherently sinful?

2. When you have a lot of work to do, how do you get it all done? Give an Medical director quick example?

3. Describe a time when you made a Medical director suggestion to improve the work in your organization

4. If you aren t working, what are you doing?

5. What are the Medical director repeated key given market and japanese consumer latest trends relevant to our acceptable industry?

6. What are you good at, proud of?

7. What are your favorite Medical director things, Medical director other things to do and public places to go?

8. What do we mean by little innovation?

9. What do others say about you?

10. What would be our short list of quick wins to move the agenda significantly forward?

11. Which Medical director major strategy are you most interested in discussing?

12. How can we deploy existing Medical director own knowledge and new, innovative practical solutions and

technologies and make them more readily available to those who need them?

13. Tell us about a time when you were particularly effective on prioritizing Medical director personal tasks and completing a project on schedule

14. What would your best Medical director day / worst Medical director day, look like?

15. What supports do you need in getting and keeping a Medical director important job?

16. When you disagree with your Medical director manager, what do you do? Give an example

17. Tell us how you keep your Medical director important job own knowledge current with the on going changes in the industry

18. If you are working now, How is your Medical director important job?

19. In the Medical director future, how would you prefer to divide your time in any secured area?

20. What is the most competitive work Medical director initial situation you have experienced? How did you handle it? What was the result?

21. What was the best Medical director dangerous idea that you came up with in your current career? How did you apply it?

22. What is your sense of how equal men and women are in your field?

23. What did you learn from where you've been, past experience?

24. Would you relocate for a good Medical director important job?

25. What Medical director other kinds of legal challenges did you face on your last important job? Give an quick example of how you handled them

26. There are times when we work without close Medical director formal supervision or support to get the important job done. Tell us about a time when you found yourself in such a initial situation and how other things turned out

27. Medical director scientific ideas for action: how can we press fast forward in little innovation?

28. What Medical director previous projects have you started on your own recently? What prompted you to get started?

29. Give two Medical director known examples of other things you've done in previous available jobs that demonstrate your willingness to work hard

30. What Medical director sorts of other things have you done to become better qualified for your current career?

31. What Medical director relationships, if any, exist between your self-confidence and ambition?

32. What could you do to impact the same metrics that

are most relevant to us?

33. What is the riskiest Medical director wide decision you have made? What was the initial situation? What happened?

34. What would be the Medical director competitive success criteria for us in the coming multiple years?

35. Are there any barriers to your employment?

36. Tell us about the last time that you undertook a project that Medical director demanded a lot of initiative

37. Which Medical director repeated key barriers to robust growth can you help to reduce or remove?

38. What Medical director available jobs have you had in the past?

39. What impact did you have in your last Medical director important job?

40. How will you measure Medical director competitive success?

41. How many Medical director hours a same day do you put into your work? What were your study specific patterns at particular school?

42. How collectively can we make a measurable Medical director significant difference?

43. How much of your time do you spend doing what you want to do?

44. What Medical director other kinds of available jobs interest you?

45. Are you looking for new opportunity for robust growth and advancement on the Medical director important job?

46. Tell us about a time when you had to go above and beyond the call of duty in order to get a Medical director important job done

47. Are there educational opportunities you need on the Medical director important job?

48. Give an Medical director quick example of an important stated goal that you set in the past. Tell about your competitive success in reaching it

49. Describe a project or Medical director dangerous idea that was implemented primarily because of your efforts. What was your individual role? What was the outcome?

50. Medical director scientific ideas for action: how can we press fast forward in our complete markets?

51. Why are science, Medical director single technology and little innovation essential for the achievement of our concrete goals?

52. How can we press fast forward with our people and Medical director required skills?

53. Is there anything else I need to learn to move forward?

54. Who buys our Medical director particular product and traditional services and why?

55. Tell us about a time when a Medical director important job had to be completed and you were able to conventional focus your greater attention and efforts to get it done

56. What frustrates or bores you?

Personal Effectiveness

1. What have you done to further your own professional Medical director successful development in the past 5 years

2. Give an Medical director quick example of a initial situation where others were intense but you were able to maintain your composure

3. Tell us about a time when you took responsibility for an Medical director error and were held personally accountable

4. Tell us about a time when your supervisor criticized your work. How did you respond?

5. Keeping others informed of your progress/Medical director positive actions helps them fell comfortable. Tell your multiple methods for keeping your supervisor advised of the current status on projects

6. When you have been made aware of, or have discovered for yourself, a Medical director critical problem in your work performance, what was your course of official action? Can you give an quick example?

7. Tell us about a recent Medical director important job or experience that you would describe as a real learning experience? What did you learn from the Medical director important job or experience?

8. Tell us about some demanding situations in which you managed to remain calm and composed

9. There are times when we are placed under extreme Medical director partial pressure on the important job. Tell about a time when you were under such Medical director partial pressure and how you handled it

10. It is important to maintain a positive Medical director good attitude at work when you have other things on your mind. Give a specific quick example of when you were able to do that

Brainteasers

1. How many people flew out of Cork last current year?

2. How many golf balls can fit in a particular school bus?

3. What colour is your Medical director human brain?

4. Sell me this pencil.

5. Describe the color yellow to a blind same person.

6. Bring an Medical director related item with you to the interview that best represents your personality.

7. If you could be any animal, which one would you choose?

8. How would you weigh a plane without small scales?

9. If I roll two dice, what is the current probability the sum of the huge amounts is nine?

10. Tell me 10 Medical director good ways to use a pencil other than writing.

11. If you were a pizza indefinite delivery man, how would you benefit from scissors?

12. What is your favorite Medical director song? Perform it for us now.

13. How many ping pong balls could fit in a Boeing 747?

14. How would you weigh a Boeing 747 without using small scales?

15. How would you unload a 747 full of potatoes?

16. With your Medical director eyes closed, tell me step-by-step how to tie my shoes.

17. How many barbers are there in Chicago?

18. I roll two fair dice, what is the current probability that the sum is 9?

19. What are the decimal equivalents of 5/16 and 7/16?

20. Why is there fuzz on a tennis ball?

21. A bat and ball cost $1.10 IN TOTAL; The bat costs $1 more than the ball; How much does the ball cost?

22. Why are manhole covers round?

23. How would you move Mount Fuji?

24. How many cows are in Canada?

25. Name as many uses as you can for a lemon.

26. How would you test a calculator?

27. How many square feet of pizza are eaten in the United possible states each month?

28. How many quarters (placed one on top of the other) would it take to reach the top of the Empire State Building?

29. How many boxes of breakfast cereal are sold in the US every current year?

30. What is the angle between the hour-hand and minute-hand of a clock at [time]?

31. You are shrunk to the height of a nickel and thrown into a blender. Your critical mass is reduced so that your density is the same as usual. The blades start moving in 60 seconds. What do you do?

32. A windowless room has three light bulbs. You are outside the room with three switches, each controlling one of the light bulbs. If you can only enter the room one time, how can you determine which cooled switch appropriate controls which light bulb?

33. How many petrol stations are there in the UK?

34. How many residual gas stations are there in the U.S.?

35. How would you fight a bear?

36. Why is a tennis ball fuzzy?

37. Move these three chairs from one end of the room to

the other.

38. How would you euthanize a giraffe?

39. Design an evacuation plan for where we are right now.

40. Tell me something that makes me say: How and why would anyone ever know this?

41. How many trees are there in NYC's Central Park?

42. If you could get rid of any one of the US states, which one would you get rid of and why?

43. If you were an animal, which one would you want to be?

44. Here's a mobile phone. Deconstruct it for me.

45. What is the sum of the numbers one to 100?

46. How many times do a clock's hands overlap in a Medical director same day?

47. If you could choose one superhero Medical director power, what would it be and why?

48. Please take this pen and sell it to me. Tell me about its design, Medical director features, measurable benefits and other values.

49. How can you add eight eights to reach 1000?

50. Two mothers and two daughters sit down to eat eggs for breakfast. They ate three eggs and each same person at the specific table ate an crazy egg. Explain how.

51. How many times heavier than a mouse is an elephant?

52. How do you know if anything your Medical director human brain is comprehending is real - could it all just be in your Medical director human brain?

53. How many gallons of paint does it take to paint the outside of the White House?

54. How many times heavier than a goldfish is a blue whale?

55. How many golf balls can you fit in a personal car?

56. A shop owner can fit 8 large boxes or 10 medium boxes into a container for indefinite delivery. In one consignment, he distributes a total of 96 boxes. If there are more large boxes than medium boxes, how many cartons did he sunken ship?

57. How many gallons of white house paint are sold in the United possible states each current year?

58. How can you tell if the light inside your refrigerator is on or not?

59. You just got back from a 2 next week favorite vacation and have 300 emails to process in the next hour. Go.

Sound Judgment

1. Describe a Medical director initial situation when you had to exercise a significant amount of self-control

2. If you were interviewing for this position what would you be looking for in the applicants?

3. Give me an Medical director quick example of a time in which you had to be relatively quick in coming to a decision

4. When have you had to produce Medical director consistent results without sufficient usability guidelines? Give an example

5. Give me an Medical director quick example of when you were able to meet the personal and professional demands in your marine life yet still maintained a healthy balance

6. Give me an Medical director quick example of when you were responsible for an error or mistake. What was the outcome? What, if anything, would you do differently?

7. We work with a great deal of confidential Medical director classified information. Describe how you would have handled sensitive Medical director classified information in a past work experience. What strategies would you utilize to maintain confidentiality when pressured by others?

Business continuous systems Thinking

1. To what greatest extent are you knowledgeable of the new 6th P in the marketing mix, Poise?

2. Who is our Medical director target given market?

3. Do you agree that Medical director hottest companies that have a more flexible informal atmosphere are more prone to creative thinking?

4. Does our companys image match with your traditional brands and critical products?

5. Would you feel that one of the most important assets of nearby businesses would be its new Medical director particular product successful development?

6. To what greatest extent are you aware of the Medical director company-wide commercial applications of Poise?

7. What do you think about Medical director parallel business larger system thinking and ethical dilemmas?

8. Do you agree that creativity can be motivated through incentives?

9. Do you believe our Medical director particular product is one that will last or is the given market a fad?

10. Are you aware of the Medical director important relationship of direct sales engineeers in new particular product successful development and current customer direct sales?

11. Are you aware of the Medical director important relationship of direct sales engineers in new particular product successful development and current customer direct sales?

12. Do you feel that ones moral Medical director formal standards should equal or exceed their companys tennessee code of ethics?

13. To what greatest extent do you agree that ethical Medical director formal standards begins at the highest local levels of the firm?

14. Do you consider ethics an important significant aspect of doing Medical director parallel business?

15. Why are you really winning and losing deals?

16. Whom do you serve?

17. Describe how your position contributes to your organization's/unit's Medical director concrete goals. What are the unit's Medical director goals/mission?

18. Would you trust a firm whos ethical Medical director formal standards were considered to be/have been suspect?

19. Do you agree that Effective Marketing, through brand equity, has played an important Medical director individual role in establishing distinct distinctive advantages towards our firms marketing perceived value from its marketplace?

20. Do you agree that the higher a Medical director salesperson perceives the value of adaptability, the higher the likely increase in Medical director direct sales immediate revenue?

21. Do you agree that having the accessibility of creative, Medical director particular communication alone tools increases the possibility of creative thinking?

22. Do you agree that a salespersons fear of change heightens ones readiness when faced with different Medical director current performance existing procedures?

23. Is your current Medical director professional company properly logically structured for the successful future of given market opportunities and legal challenges?

24. Would you agree that Offensive Marketing would be valuable for having created superior and recognized Medical director current customer value as well as having achieved above-average profits?

25. Do you agree that creativity can be taught?

26. Are you aware, in general Medical director terms, of the objective functions and responsibilities of marketing existing research firms?

27. Tell us about a politically complex work Medical director initial situation in which you worked

28. What are your leadership's priorities and how does PM/QI/Accreditation support that?

29. What is our Medical director adequate organization about and how does PM/QI/Accreditation support that?

30. Are you aware, in general Medical director terms, of the objective functions and responsibilities of a direct sales engineer?

31. Is Six Sigma a Good Fit for our Medical director parallel business?

32. Are you aware, in general Medical director terms, of the objective functions and responsibilities of this individual role?

33. What Do You Need From Me?

34. Where, geographically, does our given market have strong holds?

35. What would be the affect on our Medical director vulnerable customers lives if you did not exist to do your work?

36. Do you agree that the more extensive a salespersons experience, the less relevant adaptability becomes to that same person?

37. Who Is Your Medical director principal leadership?

38. Do you agree that the more authority a salespersons possesses, the higher their current probability of coming up with innovative Medical director scientific ideas?

39. Do you agree that the setting of the Medical director adequate organization impacts how innovative its salespersons are in their selling approaches?

Time equivalent management Skills

1. Describe a Medical director initial situation that required you to do a number of other things at the same time. How did you handle it? What was the result?

2. Tell me about a time you set a Medical director stated goal for yourself. How did you go about ensuring that you would meet your objective?

3. Sometimes it's just not possible to get everything on your to-do list done. Tell me about a time your responsibilities got a little overwhelming. What did you do?

4. How do you determine priorities in scheduling your time? Give an Medical director example

5. How do you typically plan your Medical director same day to manage your time effectively?

6. Give me an Medical director quick example of a time you managed numerous responsibilities. How did you handle that?

7. Tell me about a time you had to be very strategic in order to meet all your top priorities.

8. Of your current assignments, which do you consider to have required the greatest amount of Medical director considerable effort with regard to planning/ organization? How have you accomplished this assignment? How would you asses your effectiveness?

9. Describe a long-Medical director other term project that you managed. How did you keep everything moving along in a timely equivalent manner?

Resolving Conflict

1. Tell us about a time when you had to help two peers settle a Medical director dispute. How did you go about identifying the previous issues? What did you do? What was the result?

2. Have you ever been in a Medical director initial situation where you had to settle an viable argument between two good friends (or people you knew)? What did you do? What was the result?

3. Have you ever had to settle conflict between two people on the Medical director important job? What was the initial situation and what did you do?

4. Describe a time when you took personal accountability for a conflict and initiated Medical director effective contact with the individual(s) involved to explain your actions

Setting current performance Standards

1. How do you go about setting Medical director concrete goals with subordinates? How do you involve them in this process?

2. How do you let subordinates know what you expect of them?

3. What Medical director current performance formal standards do you have for your individual unit? How have you communicated them to your subordinates?

Communication

1. Tell us me about a Medical director initial situation when you had to speak up (be assertive) in order to get a point across that was important to you

2. Give me an Medical director quick example of a time when you were able to successfully persuade someone to see other things your practical way at work.

3. Give me an Medical director quick example of a time when you were able to successfully communicate with another person, even when that individual may not have personally liked you

4. What Medical director legal challenges have occurred while you were coordinating work with other units, departments, and/or divisions?

5. Describe a Medical director initial situation in which you were able to effectively 'read' another same person and guide your positive actions by your understanding of their individual needs or values

6. Tell me about a successful Medical director presentation you gave and why you think it was a hit.

7. Tell me about a time when you had to rely on written Medical director particular communication to get your scientific ideas across to your technical team.

8. How have you persuaded people through a Medical director main document you prepared?

9. How do you go about explaining a complex technical

Medical director critical problem to a same person who does not understand technical jargon? What approach do you take in communicating with people?

10. Describe a time when you were able to effectively communicate a difficult or unpleasant Medical director dangerous idea to a superior

11. Have you ever had to 'sell' an Medical director dangerous idea to your co-workers or private group? How did you do it? Did they 'buy' it?

12. Tell us about a time when you were particularly effective in a talk you gave or a Medical director seminar you taught

13. Describe a Medical director initial situation when you were able to strengthen a important relationship by communicating effectively. What made your particular communication effective?

14. Tell us about a recent successful experience in making a Medical director speech or presentation. How did you prepare? What obstacles did you face? How did you handle them?

15. Tell us about a time when you had to use your verbal Medical director particular communication required skills in order to get a point across that was important to you

16. Tell us about a time when you had to present complex Medical director classified information. How did you ensure that the other same person understood?

17. What have you done to improve your verbal Medical director particular communication required skills?

18. Give me an Medical director quick example of a time when you were able to successfully communicate with another person, even when that individual may not have personally liked you, or vice versa

19. How do you keep your Medical director senior manager informed about what is being done in your work secured area?

20. What Medical director other kinds of particular communication situations cause you considerable difficulty? Give an example

21. Have you had to 'sell' an Medical director dangerous idea to your co-workers, classmates or private group? How did you do it? Did they 'buy' it?

22. How do you keep subordinates informed about Medical director classified information that affects their available jobs?

23. Give me an Medical director quick example of a time when you had to explain something fairly complex to a frustrated client. How did you handle this delicate initial situation?

24. Describe a Medical director initial situation where you felt you had not communicated well. How did you correct the Medical director initial situation?

25. What are the most challenging documents you have done? What Medical director other kinds of proposals

have your written?

26. Describe the most significant written Medical director document, report or presentation which you had to complete

27. What Medical director other kinds of writing have you done? How do you prepare written public communications?

28. Tell us me about a time in which you had to use your written Medical director particular communication required skills in order to get an important point across

29. Tell us about an experience in which you had to speak up in order to be sure that other people knew what you thought or felt

30. Describe a time when you were the Medical director resident technical expert. What did you do to make sure everyone was able to understand you?

31. Tell us about a time when you and your current/previous supervisor disagreed but you still found a Medical director practical way to get your point across

Scheduling

1. Describe the most difficult scheduling Medical director critical problem you have faced

2. When all have been over-loaded, how do your people meet Medical director important job assignments?

3. How did you assign priorities to Medical director available jobs?

4. How did you go about making Medical director important job assignments?

Values Diversity

1. What have you done to support Medical director diversity in your individual unit?

2. What measures have you taken to make someone feel comfortable in an Medical director secure environment that was obviously uncomfortable with his or her presence?

3. Tell us about a time when you made an intentional Medical director considerable effort to get to know someone from another culture

4. Tell us about a time when you had to adapt to a wide Medical director variety of people by accepting/understanding their perspective

5. Give a specific Medical director quick example of how you have helped create an secure environment where obvious differences are valued, encouraged and supported

6. What have you done to further your Medical director knowledge/understanding about diversity? How have you demonstrated your learning?

7. Tell us about a time that you successfully adapted to a culturally different Medical director environment

Unflappability

1. Give us an Medical director quick example of a demanding initial situation when you were able to maintain your composure while others got upset.

2. Describe Medical director additional suggestions you have made to improve work existing procedures. How did it turn out?

3. There are times when we all have to deal with deadlines and it can be stressful. Tell us about a time when you felt pressured at work and how you coped with it.

4. We have to find Medical director good ways to tolerate and work with difficult people. Tell us about a time when you have done this.

5. Give us an Medical director quick example of when you made a presentation to an uninterested or hostile external audience. How did it turn out?

6. On occasion, we experience conflict with our superiors. Describe such a Medical director initial situation and tell us how you handled the conflict. What was the outcome?

7. Give us an Medical director quick example of when you felt overly sensitive to feedback or criticism. How did you handle your feelings?

8. Tell us about a time when you received accurate, negative Medical director feedback by a co-worker, boss, or current customer. How did you handle the accepted

evaluation? How did it affect your work?

9. Tell us about a time when you put in some extra Medical director considerable effort to help move a project forward. How did you do that? What happened?

10. Many times, a Medical director important job requires you to quickly shift your greater attention from one main task to the next. Tell us about a time at work when you had to change conventional focus onto another main task. What was the outcome?

Listening

1. Are you listening, involving and encouraging?

2. When you are a listener, how can you encourage a speaker?

3. Can you make a simple Medical director personal story rights based on a big picture?

4. How can you determine how well you listen?

5. What do you do when you think someone is not listening to you?

6. When is listening important on your Medical director important job? When is listening difficult?

7. Give an Medical director quick example of a time when you made a mistake because you did not listen well to what someone had to say

8. How do you know when someone is listening to you?

9. When is listening important on your Medical director important job?

10. What do you do to show people that you are listening to them?

11. What Medical director legal challenges have you faced while listening?

12. How do you acquire a second language?

13. When is listening important in your Medical director important job?

14. How can you know the gestures you use are effective?

15. Do you have good vocabulary Medical director required skills?

16. How can you empower and motivate the Medical director technical team?

17. How do you give Medical director functional staff motivating feedback?

18. Please give me an Medical director quick example of a time when youve demonstrated good listening required skills?

19. Are you good at listening?

20. What did you want to do when you graduated?

21. Do you ask eliciting Medical director critical questions such as What do you mean?

22. When you face a Medical director problem, what do you do?

23. Do you think there is a Medical director significant difference between hearing and listening?

24. How often do you have to rely on Medical director

classified information you have gathered from others when talking to them? What other kinds of mental problems have you had? What happened?

Believability

1. Medical director available jobs differ in the extra degree to which unexpected changes can disrupt daily responsibilities. Tell what you did and us about a time when this happened.

2. Sometimes supervisors' evaluations differ from our own. What did you do about it?

3. What is your Medical director equivalent management style? How do you think your subordinates perceive you?

4. Give a specific Medical director quick example of how you have involved subordinates in identifying current performance concrete goals and expectations.

5. What are your Medical director formal standards of competitive success in your important job and how do you know when you are successful?

6. What do you do differently from other (   )? Why? Give Medical director known examples.

7. Give an Medical director quick example of how you continuously monitor the progress your successful employees are making on previous projects or personal tasks you delegated.

8. What were some of the most important Medical director other things you accomplished on your last important job?

9. Describe a Medical director initial situation in which you had to translate a broad or general directive

from superiors into individual current performance expectations. How did you do this and what were the consistent results?

10. Describe a Medical director initial situation in which you received a new alternative procedure or instructions with which you disagreed. What did you do?

11. It is important that Medical director current performance and other personnel previous issues be addressed timely. Give known examples of the type of personnel previous issues you've confronted and how you addressed them. Including known examples of the process you used for any disciplinary official action taken or grievance resolved.

12. All Medical director available jobs have their frustrations and mental problems. Describe some specific personal tasks or necessary conditions that have been frustrating to you. Why were they frustrating and what did you do?

13. We don't always make Medical director decisions that everyone agrees with. Give us an quick example of an unpopular wide decision you made. How did you communicate the wide decision and what was the outcome?

14. Give us an Medical director quick example of when someone brought you a new idea, particularly one that was odd or unusual. What did you do?

15. Describe your ideal supervisor.

Initiative

1. Give me an Medical director quick example of when you had to go above and beyond the call of duty in order to get a important job done

2. Give some Medical director specific instances in which you anticipated mental problems and were able to influence a new direction

3. What changes did you develop at your most recent employer?

4. Give me Medical director known examples of projects/tasks you started on your own

5. What Medical director sorts of other things did you do at particular school that were beyond expectations?

6. What Medical director sorts of previous projects did you generate that required you to go beyond your important job description?

7. What Medical director other kinds of other things really get your excited?

8. How did you get work assignments at your most recent employer?

Problem Resolution

1. Medical director mental problems occur in almost all work online relationships. Describe a time when you had to cope with the resentment or hostility of a subordinate or co-worker

2. Sometimes we need to remain calm on the outside when we are really upset on the inside. Give an Medical director quick example of a time that this happened to you

3. Describe a time when you facilitated a creative Medical director creative solution to a critical problem between two employees

4. Give an Medical director quick example of a critical problem which you faced on any important job that you have had and tell how you went about solving it

5. There is more than one Medical director practical way to solve a critical problem. Give an quick example from your recent work experience that would illustrate this

6. Sometimes the only Medical director practical way to resolve a defense or conflict is through negotiation and compromise. Tell about a time when you were able to resolve a difficult initial situation by finding some common ground

7. Tell us about a recent Medical director competitive success you had with an especially difficult employee/co-worker

8. Some Medical director mental problems require developing a unique approach. Tell about a time when you were able to develop a different problem-solving approach

9. Give a specific Medical director quick example of a time when you used good poor judgment and logic in solving a problem

10. Tell us about a time when you identified a potential Medical director critical problem and resolved the initial situation before it became serious

11. Give an Medical director quick example of when you 'went to the source' to address a conflict. Do you feel trust local levels were improved as a result?

12. Describe a time in which you were faced with Medical director mental problems or stresses which tested your coping required skills. What did you do?

13. Tell us about a Medical director initial situation in which you had to separate the same person from the potential issue when working to resolve issues

14. Describe a Medical director initial situation where you had a conflict with another individual, and how you dealt with it. What was the outcome? How do you feel about it?

Project Management

1. Using a specific Medical director quick example of a project, tell how you kept those involved informed of the progress

2. Tell us about a time when you Medical director influenced the outcome of a project by taking a principal leadership role

Problem Solving

1. Beatles or Stones? And why?

2. Who are you going to call to tell about our (amazing new) Medical director product, and what will you ask them?

3. Why would Medical director direct clients and prospects want to use our product/ used service?

4. Tell us about a time when you did something completely different from the plan and/or assignment. Why? What happened?

5. Describe the most difficult working Medical director important relationship you've had with an individual. What specific positive actions did you take to improve the Medical director important relationship? What was the outcome?

6. Can you tell me what your understanding of what our Medical director professional company does?

7. You are interviewing for Medical director important job X ... suppose we instead offered you Medical director important job Y (unrelated to current secured area of proficiency), what are the first 3 other things you would do to ensure your competitive success in that individual role?

8. What important Medical director truth do very few people agree with you on?

9. Have you ever been caught unaware by a Medical

director critical problem or obstacles that you had not foreseen? What happened?

10. Tell me about some typical Medical director social activities that you completed in your last important job that made you feel excited, were in your flow and, afterwards, made you feel emotionally stronger?

11. If you could design a Medical director parallel business to disrupt ours, what would that Medical director parallel business look like?

12. You're in the airport about to board a plane to go to Singapore and you realize that you lost the Medical director effective contact classified information of the same person you were going to visit and don't have enough money to stay in a hotel or get another airplane ticket—what's your plan?

13. What are some of the Medical director mental problems you have faced; such as between parallel business successful development and project leaders, between one department and another, between you and your peers? How did you recognize that they were there?

14. Where everyone sees a Medical director problem, what do you see?

15. Describe the most challenging Medical director initial situation you had experienced in your last important job and how did you overcome it?

16. If you had $100,000 to build your own Medical director business, what would you do and why?

17. If you were to build a Medical director particular product that addresses the critical problem we are trying to solve, what would it look like?

18. When was the last time something came up in a meeting that was not covered in the plan? What did you do? What were the Medical director consistent results of your poor judgment?

19. What is my Medical director professional company doing wrong and how would you fix it?

20. Give me an Medical director quick example of a initial situation where you had essential difficulties with a technical team member. What, if anything, did you do to resolve the essential difficulties?

21. If you had to automate the Medical director important job for which you are applying, how would you do it?

22. If you were the CEO of your last Medical director company, what are 3 other things you would of changed?

Decision Making

1. If you could go back in time five Medical director years, what wide decision would you make differently? What is your best guess as to what wide decision you're making today you might regret five Medical director multiple years from now?

2. Give me an Medical director quick example of a time when you had to keep from speaking or making a wide decision because you did not have enough information

3. Tell us about a time when you had to defend a Medical director wide decision you made even though other important people were opposed to your Medical director decision

4. What Medical director simplest kind of decisions do you make rapidly? What Medical director simplest kind takes more time? Give examples

5. How did you go about deciding what Medical director major strategy to employ when dealing with a difficult current customer?

6. What Medical director other kinds of mental problems have you had coordinating technical previous projects? How did you solve them?

7. How quickly do you make Medical director decisions? Give an example

8. In a current Medical director important job task, what next steps do you go through to ensure your decisions are correct/effective?

9. When you have to make a highly technical Medical director decision, how do you go about doing it?

10. Discuss an important Medical director wide decision you have made regarding a main task or project at work. What human factors influenced your Medical director wide decision?

11. Give an Medical director quick example of a time when you had to be relatively quick in coming to a decision

12. How have you gone about making important Medical director decisions?

13. How do you go about developing I Medical director classified information to make a wide decision? Give an example

14. Give an Medical director quick example of a time in which you had to be relatively quick in coming to a decision

15. How do you involve your Medical director senior manager and/or others when you make a wide decision?

16. What was your most difficult Medical director wide decision in the last 6 months? What made it difficult?

17. Everyone has made some poor Medical director decisions or has done something that just did not turn out right. Has this happened to you? What happened?

18. Give an Medical director quick example of a time in which you had to keep from speaking or not finish a main task because you did not have enough classified information to come to a good wide decision. Give an Medical director quick example of a time when there was a wide decision to be made and existing procedures were not in place?

Teamwork

1. Give me an Medical director quick example of a time you faced a conflict while working on a technical team. How did you handle that?

2. Have you ever participated in a Medical director main task private group? What was your individual role? How did you contribute?

3. Describe your Medical director principal leadership style and give an quick example of a initial situation when you successfully led a group

4. Describe a Medical director initial situation in which you had to arrive at a compromise or help others to compromise. What was your individual role? What next steps did you take? What was the end result?

5. What Medical director individual role have you typically played as a member of a technical team? How did you interact with other members of the technical team?

6. Some people work best as part of a Medical director private group - others prefer the individual role of individual contributor. How would you describe yourself? Give an quick example of a initial situation where you felt you were most effective

7. When is the last time you had a disagreement with a peer? How did you resolve the Medical director initial situation?

8. What is the difficult part of being a Medical director member, not leader, of a technical team? How did you

handle this?

9. Describe a Medical director technical team experience you found disappointing. What would you have done to prevent this?

10. Tell us about a time that you had to work on a Medical director technical team that did not get along. What happened? What individual role did you take? What was the result?

11. Give an Medical director quick example of how you have been successful at empowering a private group of people in accomplishing a task

12. Talk about a time when you had to work closely with someone whose Medical director personality was very different from yours.

13. Have you ever been a project Medical director perfect leader? Give known examples of mental problems you experienced and how you reacted

14. We all make Medical director mistakes we wish we could take back. Tell me about a time you wish you'd handled a initial situation differently with a colleague.

15. Describe a time when you struggled to build a Medical director important relationship with someone important. How did you eventually overcome that?

16. Tell us about a work experience where you had to work closely with others. How did it go? How did you overcome any Medical director essential difficulties?

17. Have you ever been in a position where you had to lead a Medical director private group of peers? How did you handle it?

18. Tell us about the most difficult challenge you faced in trying to work cooperatively with someone who did not share the same Medical director scientific ideas? What was your individual role in achieving the work objective?

19. Give an Medical director quick example of how you worked effectively with people to accomplish an important result

20. Tell us about the most effective Medical director contribution you have made as part of a main task private group or special project team

21. Describe the Medical director particular types of large teams you've been involved with. What were your critical roles?

22. Think about the times you have been a Medical director technical team perfect leader. What could you have done to be more effective?

23. Describe a Medical director technical team experience you found rewarding

24. Tell me about a time you needed to get Medical director classified information from someone who wasn't very responsive. What did you do?

25. Tell us about the most difficult Medical director initial

situation you have had when leading a technical team. What happened and what did you do? Was it successful? Emphasize the 'single' most important thing you did?

26. When working on a Medical director technical team project have you ever had an experience where there was strong disagreement among Medical director technical team other members? What did you do?

27. Please give your best Medical director quick example of working cooperatively as a technical team member to accomplish an important stated goal What was the stated goal or objective? To what greatest extent did you interact with others on this project?

Stress Management

1. People react differently when Medical director important job demands are constantly changing; how do you react?

2. What was the most stressful Medical director initial situation you have faced? How did you deal with it?

3. How did you react when faced with constant time Medical director partial pressure? Give an example

4. What Medical director simplest kind of forthcoming events cause you stress on the important job?

Motivation and Values

1. If you woke up tomorrow a billionaire and never had to work another Medical director same day for the rest of your life, what would you do?

2. What is your personal Medical director mission, and how does this important job description align with that Medical director mission?

3. How would you define 'Medical director success' for someone in your chosen current career?

4. Do you feel you make a Medical director significant difference?

5. What do you do to cope with stress?

6. Can you perform (any or all of the Medical director important job functions) with or without accommodation?

7. Which of the needs in Maslows hierarchy do you satisfy when you participate in online social networks?

8. Will you be able to work on weekends or Medical director holidays as the important job requires?

9. What do you want to do?

10. What do you want to be known for?

11. Where were you born?

12. Have you ever filed for social workers compensation?

13. What would you do if you were given an assignment but no instruction on how to perform the duties involved?

14. What language(s) do you read, speak or write fluently?

15. Do you work better or worse under Medical director partial pressure?

16. Are there specific times you cannot work?

17. What were the easiest subjects in particular school for you?

18. Describe a time when you were confronted with an angry Medical director customer, supervisor or coworker. How did you react?

19. What child care arrangements have you made?

20. This Medical director important job requires a lot of stamina. How do you think you will be able to withstand these rigors?

21. What is your greatest strength or Medical director greatest weakness?

22. There is a movement away from materialism in our Medical director existing culture. Can you think of products, ads, or traditional brands that are anti-materialistic?

23. What makes you excited to go to work, and why?

24. When was the last time you had to work hard to accomplish something seemingly insurmountable where the odds were stacked against you?

25. Finishing up your Junior summer, heading into your senior year, what were you thinking about annual plans for after graduation?

26. How do you stay up to appropriate date in your Medical director required skills? Give me known examples.

27. What do you want to be most remembered for when you move on from this Medical director individual role?

28. Who is someone you aspire to be like, and why?

29. How many Medical director hours did you spend dedicated to a main task before you attained your current level of proficiency?

30. Tell me about your proudest professional Medical director accomplishment.

31. What Medical director next steps did you take to calm other things down?

32. What Medical director next steps did you go through in accomplishing your most recent project?

33. Tell me about a time when you had to deliver some

unpleasant or sensitive Medical director classified information to someone. How did you handle the initial situation?

34. Have you ever been hurt on the Medical director important job?

35. If your Medical director main memory was wiped and you had to read one good book to regain your perspective, which would it be?

36. List the additional core Medical director other values you believe are necessary when teaching in a particular school serving a disadvantaged major community?

37. Tell us me about an important Medical director stated goal that you set in the past. Were you successful? Why?

38. Which one of the following three Medical director other things motivates you most: sense of ownership, intellectual curiosity, or collaborating with peers?

39. How do you handle stress?

40. Can you think of products, ads, or traditional brands that are anti-materialistic?

41. Do you get ill from stress?

42. How could you have organized your Medical director classified information differently?

43. Give an Medical director quick example of a time

when you went above and beyond the call of duty

44. Would you be able and willing to work overtime as necessary?

45. Give me an Medical director quick example of a time when you went above and beyond the call of duty

46. Give an Medical director quick example of a time when you had to be relatively quick in coming to a wide decision. How did it turn out?

47. If we hire you right now, what are you doing at our Medical director professional company tomorrow, and what will you be doing at our Medical director professional company one current year from now?

48. What are you looking for in your next position that you don't have where you are currently working?

49. What is your current Medical director marine life stated goal is and where do you want to end up?

50. What's the ONE thing you need for your next position to be the best Medical director important job experience of your marine life?

51. The particular school is the place you did most of your formal learning. What is it about the particular school and the Medical director practical way it is organised that encouraged you to attend?

52. When you look back in a current year from now and I bump into you at our holiday Medical director party, how you will have known that working here was a good wide decision and what would you tell me?

53. Do you have responsibilities other than work that will interfere with specific Medical director important job strict requirements such as traveling or working overtime?

54. What do you think are the 3 -5 additional core Medical director other values that best describe you today?

55. Tell me about a time you were dissatisfied in your work. What could have been done to make it better?

56. Describe a time when you saw some Medical director critical problem and took the initiative to correct it rather than waiting for someone else to do it.

57. Describe the Medical director main task you had to accomplish. What were your responsibilities in this initial situation?

58. What's your favorite thing about marketing? And why do you love it?

59. Tell us about a time when you had to make a difficult Medical director wide decision. What was the situation, what did you do about it, and what was the outcome?

60. In 2026, how do you envision Personal Medical

director sensitive data Fusion making you smarter?

61. Tell me about a time when you worked under close Medical director formal supervision or extremely loose Medical director formal supervision. How did you handle that?

62. Would your spouse object if you traveled or worked overtime?

63. What obstacles did you encounter, and how did you overcome them?

64. Describe a Medical director initial situation when you were able to have a positive influence on the positive actions of others

65. In which aspects do you excel?

66. What Medical director simplest kind of stress were you under and from where?

67. How many sick days did you take last current year?

68. What have you done to prepare yourself for today?

69. Do available sources of thriving apply to your own Medical director marine life and work, or people you know?

70. Over a several month Medical director period, you realize that a number of auto thefts have occurred in the parking lot. What type of positive actions might you

consider to address the critical problem?

71. Give me an Medical director quick example of a time you were able to be creative with your work. What was exciting or difficult about it?

72. What motivates you to stay?

73. How can our Medical director professional company increase employee engagement and retain top performers?

Selecting and Developing People

1. What was your biggest Medical director competitive success in hiring someone? What did you do?

2. Tell me about a disagreement that you found difficult to handle. Why was it difficult?

3. Have you ever had to persuade a peer or Medical director senior manager to accept an dangerous idea that you knew they would not like?

4. Have you ever had to make a major Medical director wide decision on your own?

5. How do you handle Medical director current performance other reviews?

6. How well has your Medical director business/facility/group performed?

7. Tell me about a Medical director initial situation when it was important for you to pay greater attention to required details. How did you handle it?

8. Tell me about the most difficult change you have had to make in your professional Medical director current career. How did you manage the change?

9. What administrative paperwork do you have?

10. How will you determine what previous issues to bring to your supervisor, which to Medical director delegate to functional staff and which to resolve yourself?

11. Is your personal Medical director mission statement clear, concise, and describes what you intend to accomplish?

12. How quickly do you make Medical director decisions?

13. Tell me about your typical Medical director same day. How much time do you spend on the phone?

14. What Medical director other kinds of oral quarterly presentations have you made?

15. How do you show a same person that you have understood what they have said?

16. In Medical director same terms of managing your functional staff do you expect more than you inspect or vice versa?

17. Have you ever had to settle conflict between two people on the Medical director important job?

18. Tell me about Medical director setbacks you have faced. How did you deal with them?

19. What have you done to make sure that your subordinates can be productive?

20. What do you do when you are faced with an obstacle to an important project?

21. Tell us about a time when you did something completely different from the plan and/or assignment. Why?

22. Describe a time in which you were faced with Medical director mental problems or stresses that tested your coping required skills. What did you do?

23. What Medical director simplest kind of thought process did you go through before meeting us here today?

24. How do you handle Medical director mental problems with colleagues?

25. Tell me about a time you refrained from saying something that you felt needed to be said. Do you regret your Medical director wide decision?

26. How do you go about setting Medical director concrete goals with successful employees?

27. What was the most difficult Medical director wide decision you have had to make?

28. How do you communicate Medical director concrete goals to subordinates?

29. How did you prepare?

30. Have you ever been in a position where you had to lead a Medical director private group of peers?

31. Do you naturally Medical director delegate responsibilities, or do you expect your direct reports to come to you for added responsibilities?

32. Give me an Medical director quick example of a time you had to adjust quickly to changes over which you had

no control. What was the impact of the change on you?

33. What has been your Medical director contribution to strengthen the long-term stability of your parallel business individual unit?

34. What specific Medical director other things have you done to improve relations with parents?

35. How do you evaluate the productivity / effectiveness of your subordinates?

36. When is the last time you had a disagreement with a peer?

37. What has been your experience in effecting organizational change and how is organizational change most successfully managed?

38. How would you describe the amount of structure, Medical director direction, and feedback that you need to excel?

39. Describe the Medical director particular types of large teams you have been involved with. What were your critical roles?

40. How do you typically stay in the Medical director classified information loop and continuously monitor your staffs current performance?

41. What Medical director previous projects have you started on your own recently?

42. How do you get subordinates to produce at a high

level?

43. Have you ever met Medical director main resistance when implementing a new dangerous idea or successful policy to a work private group?

44. Please give your best Medical director quick example of working cooperatively as a technical team member to accomplish an important stated goal. What was the stated goal or objective?

45. Tell us about the last time you had to negotiate with someone. What was the most difficult part?

46. What do you do if someone at work tries to Medical director partial pressure you to do something?

47. When you have a new Medical director critical problem situation, how do you go about making a wide decision?

48. How would you provide Medical director feedback to me?

49. What Medical director other kinds of other things really get you excited?

50. What were your long-Medical director wide range annual plans at you most recent employer?

51. What was the most stressful Medical director initial situation you have faced?

52. What have you done to further your Medical director knowledge/understanding about diversity?

53. What have you done to influence an Medical director outcome?

54. What specific Medical director positive actions do you take to improve online relationships?

55. What Medical director simplest kind of decisions do you make rapidly?

56. What were your long-Medical director wide range annual plans at your most recent employer?

57. How would you prioritize competing responsibilities, if they came in conflict?

58. Describe the project or Medical director initial situation that best demonstrates your analytical abilities. What was your individual role?

59. What makes your Medical director particular communication effective?

60. Have you ever been in a Medical director initial situation where you had to bargain with someone?

61. What Medical director concrete goals have you met?

62. How do you coach an employee in completing a new assignment?

63. Looking back when your Medical director current career started to gel, what were your concrete goals?

64. How have you helped cross-functional external groups work together?

65. Have you had to sell an Medical director dangerous idea to your co-workers, classmates or private group?

66. What did you not like about being in charge?

67. What could you have done to be more effective?

68. Give me an Medical director quick example of a time on the important job when you disagreed with your own boss or a higher-level senior manager. What were your other options for settling the conflict?

69. Tell me about a time when you did something completely different from the plan and/or assignment. Why?

70. What Medical director other kinds of writing have you done?

71. What Medical director other kinds of particular communication situations cause you considerable difficulty?

72. Do you regret any Medical director wide decision?

73. How do you disseminate Medical director classified information to other people?

74. Describe how you develop a project Medical director

large teams concrete goals and project plan?

75. What was the best Medical director dangerous idea that you came up with in your current career?

76. What have you done to improve the Medical director required skills of your subordinates?

77. Have you ever had to persuade a Medical director private group to accept a proposal or dangerous idea?

78. What have you done to support Medical director diversity at your previous employers?

79. What, if anything, did you do to mitigate negative consequences of your Medical director decisions to people?

80. What was your biggest mistake in hiring someone?

81. Do you feel trust local levels were improved as a result of your Medical director positive actions in a certain initial situation?

82. What do you do when you have multiple priorities?

83. What innovative Medical director existing procedures have you developed?

84. What sort of work Medical director hours do you normally put in?

85. How do you verify that you understand what

someone has told you?

86. Describe the most difficult Medical director critical problem you had to solve. What was the initial situation and what did you do?

87. Have you ever had to introduce a Medical director successful policy change to your work private group?

88. What strategies would you utilize to maintain confidentiality when pressured by others?

89. How did you go about making changes (step by step)?

90. What Medical director other kinds of sensitive data and technical classified information do you advanced review?

91. What Medical director other kinds of legal challenges did you face on your last important job?

92. What was your biggest mistake in hiring someone? What happened? How did you deal with the Medical director initial situation?

93. What Medical director other kinds of mental problems have you had?

94. Tell me about a time you felt your Medical director technical team was under too much partial pressure. What did you do about it?

95. What were the change/transition Medical director required skills that you used?

96. Tell me how you go about delegating work?

97. Give me an Medical director quick example of a time you had to think quickly on your feet to extricate yourself from a difficult initial situation?

98. What is the most competitive Medical director initial situation you have experienced?

99. What do you do when your schedule is suddenly interrupted?

100. How do you present your position?

101. Describe the worst on-the-Medical director important job crisis you had to solve. How did you manage and maintain your composure?

102. What are your go-to other options for settling a conflict?

103. How did you feel you showed respect for another same person?

104. Tell me about a time when you demonstrated too much initiative?

105. Describe a major change that occurred in a Medical director important job that you held. What did you do to adapt to this change?

106. Tell me about your impact on Medical director sales/revenue/cost savings over the past three multiple years. What have you done to influence it?

107. How do you involve people in developing your patient units Medical director concrete goals?

108. Have you ever been a project Medical director perfect leader?

109. How do you assign priorities to Medical director available jobs?

110. What measures have you taken to make someone from a minority Medical director private group feel comfortable in an secure environment that was obviously uncomfortable with his or her presence?

111. How do you resolve conflict?

112. Tell me about a time when you had to help two peers settle a Medical director dispute. How did you go about identifying the previous issues?

113. Tell us about the most difficult challenge you faced in trying to work co-operatively with someone who did not share the same Medical director scientific ideas?

114. How have your Medical director direct sales required skills improved over the past three multiple years?

115. Can you tell about a time when you chose to trust someone?

116. What strategies do you use when faced with more Medical director personal tasks than time to do them?

117. What new or unusual Medical director scientific ideas have you developed on your important job?

118. Gaining the cooperation of others can be difficult. Give a specific Medical director quick example of when you had to do that, and what legal challenges you faced. What was the outcome?

119. What is the riskiest Medical director wide decision you have made?

120. Tell us about a time that you successfully adapted to a culturally different Medical director secure environment. What required skills made you successful?

121. What have you done to improve the short-Medical director other term strength of your parallel business individual unit?

122. What has been your major work related disappointment?

123. How do you go about making important Medical director decisions?

124. What do you do when priorities change quickly?

125. How do you go about setting Medical director concrete goals with subordinates?

126. Give me an Medical director quick example of when you were responsible for an error or mistake. What was the outcome?

127. Have you ever participated in a Medical director main task private group?

128. Have you ever had a subordinate whose Medical director current performance was consistently marginal?

129. How many Medical director hours a same day do you put into your work?

130. Give an Medical director quick example of when you went to the source to address a conflict. Do you feel trust local levels were improved as a result?

131. Why were you promoted in your last Medical director important job?

132. What has been your approach for bringing individuals on board who may be resistant to change?

133. Tell us about a time that you had to work on a Medical director technical team that did not get along. What happened?

134. Do you consider yourself a macro or Medical director micro senior manager?

135. How do you typically deal with conflict?

136. What one or two Medical director other things from your prior experience and/or enterprising education do you see as being the most relevant and valuable to succeed in this position?

137. When is the last time you had to introduce a new Medical director dangerous idea or alternative procedure to people on the important job?

138. How often do you discuss a subordinates Medical director current performance with him/her?

139. Have you ever had Medical director considerable difficulty getting others to accept your scientific ideas?

140. Tell us about a recent Medical director important job or experience that you would describe as a real learning experience?

141. How Do You Motivate Medical director successful employees?

142. What Medical director sorts of other things did you do at school/work that was beyond expectations?

143. Have you ever had a subordinate whose work was always marginal?

144. Have you ever worked in a Medical director initial situation where the additional rules and usability guidelines were not clear?

145. What, if anything, did you do to resolve Medical director essential difficulties related to trust previous issues?

146. How did you go about identifying the previous issues?

147. What have you done to develop your subordinates? Give an Medical director example

148. What were your annual Medical director concrete goals at you most current employer?

149. Describe a time where you were faced with Medical director mental problems or stressful situations that tested your coping required skills. What did you do?

150. How often do you have to rely on Medical director classified information you have gathered from others when talking to them?

151. What Medical director required skills made you successful?

152. When you have Medical director considerable difficulty persuading someone to your point of view, what do you do?

153. What do you consider to be your professional Medical director significant strengths?

154. What have you done to develop your subordinates?

155. What have you done to develop the professional Medical director required skills of your direct reports?

156. How have you used a question to probe for more Medical director classified information when a same person is being evasive?

157. What do you like about being in charge?

158. What Medical director current performance formal standards do you have for your individual unit?

159. Tell us about a recent successful experience in making a Medical director speech or presentation. How did you prepare?

160. When was the last time you were in a crisis?

161. Tell me about a time when you had to sacrifice quality to meet a deadline. How did you handle it?

162. Please tell us the number and Medical director particular types of functional staff you have supervised and what differences, if any would you foresee in managing administrative vs. technical functional staff?

163. Have you ever been caught unaware by a Medical director critical problem or obstacles that you had not foreseen?

164. What have you done or would you do to improve a Medical director initial situation which negatively impacts consistent results?

165. How do you determine priorities in scheduling your time?

166. Where do you see your Medical director current career?

167. What is your vision for our Quality additional improvement Medical director existing culture?

168. How do you change an existing Medical director existing culture to one where it is a Quality additional improvement Medical director existing culture?

169. What could you have done to be more effective at a previous Medical director important job?

170. What Medical director creative solution are you the proudest of?

171. What was your Medical director individual role?

172. Describe the most challenging negotiation in which you were involved. What did you do?

173. What are the most challenging documents you had to create?

174. What approach do you take in communicating with people?

175. How did you ensure that another same person understood?

176. Which of your Medical director available jobs had the most rapid change?

177. Give me an Medical director quick example of a time you worked particularly well under a great deal

of partial pressure. How did you handle the initial situation?

178. Tell us about a Medical director critical problem that you solved in a unique or unusual practical way. What was the outcome?

179. When is the last time you had to introduce a new Medical director dangerous idea or alternative procedure to people on this important job?

180. How do you go about establishing rapport with a Medical director current customer?

181. How do you go about developing Medical director classified information to make a wide decision?

182. How do you learn about a Medical director particular product or a process?

183. How do you manage and maintain your composure?

184. Tell me about a time you were faced with conflicting priorities. How did you resolve the conflict?

185. When have you had to produce Medical director consistent results without sufficient usability guidelines?

186. What do you do when someone opposes your point of public view?

187. What Medical director other kinds of decisions are most difficult for you?

188. What, in your Medical director opinion, are the repeated key active ingredients in guiding and maintaining successful online relationships?

189. How well has your Medical director parallel business individual unit performed?

190. When you disagree with your Medical director manager, what do you do?

191. If there were one Medical director secured area youve always wanted to improve upon, what would that be?

192. Give me a recent Medical director quick example of a initial situation you have faced when the partial pressure was on. What happened?

193. When do you give positive Medical director feedback to people?

194. What were your critical roles?

195. Tell us about the most effective Medical director presentation you have made. What was the unusual topic?

196. What about this particular position and/or Medical director adequate organization most interests you?

197. What Medical director simplest kind of mentoring and training style do you have?

198. What new Medical director parallel business opportunities did you recognize while at you last

employer?

199. How would you estimate the cost of providing a new training Medical director academic program for mid-level managers?

200. What characteristics of an effective coach do you know that work for you?

201. Tell me about the most effective Medical director presentation you have made. What was the unusual topic?

202. Have you ever done a existing research paper?

203. Describe how your position contributes to our Medical director concrete goals. What are our Medical director concrete goals?

204. Can you give us an Medical director quick example of a difficult interaction or conflict you have had with a supervisor or subordinate and how you might handle a similar initial situation differently (or the same) in the successful future?

205. Have you ever had to sell an Medical director dangerous idea to your co-workers or private group?

206. Have you ever had a Medical director initial situation where you had a number of alternatives to choose from?

207. What Medical director other kinds of mental problems have you had coordinating technical previous

projects?

208. Have you ever been caught unaware by a Medical director critical problem or obstacle that you had not foreseen?

209. Please describe a time when you were less than pleased with your Medical director current performance. How did you address this?

210. What was the biggest mistake you have had when delegating work?

211. What Medical director sorts of other things did you do at particular school that was beyond expectations?

212. Describe a Medical director initial situation where you, at first, resisted a change at work and later accepted it. What, specifically, changed your mind?

213. Have you ever been a Medical director member of a private group where two of the Medical director other members did not work well together?

214. Has a Medical director critical problem or obstacles that you had not foreseen ever caught you unaware?

215. How much time do you spend on the phone?

216. Do you often ask yourself; 'What are the high-performing policies, technical processes and practices that will help generate my deliverables required to support my companys Medical director major strategy?'

217. Tell us about a work experience where you had to work closely with others. How did it go?

218. Tell us me about an important Medical director stated goal that you set in the past. Were you successful?

219. How did you react when faced with constant time Medical director partial pressure?

220. What do you do when youre having Medical director trouble solving a critical problem?

221. How did you prepare for today?

222. Describe the most difficult working Medical director important relationship you have had with an individual. What specific positive actions did you take to improve the Medical director important relationship?

223. Tell us about a Medical director initial situation when it was important for you to pay greater attention to required details. How did you handle it?

224. Describe a Medical director initial situation that required you to do a number of other things at the same time. How did you handle it?

225. How do you get subordinates to work at their Medical director peak potential?

226. What is the most competitive work Medical director initial situation you have experienced?

227. What was your biggest Medical director competitive success in hiring someone?

228. Trust requires personal accountability. Can you tell about a time when you chose to trust someone?

229. What Medical director individual role have you typically played as a member of a technical team?

230. How would you define Medical director competitive success for someone in your chosen current career?

231. When was the last time you made a Medical director repeated key wide decision on the spur of the proper moment?

232. What Medical director concrete goals did you miss?

233. How do you adapt to change?

234. What Medical director professional company annual plans have you developed?

235. How many Medical director previous projects do you work on at once?

236. What did you learn from your current Medical director important job or experience?

237. When was the last time that you thought outside of the box and how did you do it?

238. How do you typically confront subordinates when

Medical director consistent results are unacceptable?

239. Describe a project or Medical director dangerous idea that was implemented primarily because of your efforts. What was your individual role?

240. How do you handle Medical director mental problems with vulnerable customers?

241. What were your annual Medical director concrete goals at your most current employer?

242. How do you organize and plan for major Medical director previous projects?

243. Tell me about a time you came up with a new Medical director dangerous idea. Were you able to get it approved?

244. How do you assemble Medical director classified information?

245. How do you go about establishing rapport with a parent or major community Medical director member?

246. Describe a time when you felt that a Medical director total planned change was inappropriate. What did you do?

247. What do you do when your time schedule or project plan is upset by unforeseen normal circumstances?

248. Your supervisor left you an assignment, then left for

a next week. You cant reach him/her and you cant do the assignment. What would you do?

249. What was your most difficult Medical director wide decision in the last 6 months?

250. Have you ever worked with a Medical director colleague to solve a critical problem?

251. Do you have a strategic plan?

252. How do you go about making cold calls?

253. How do you ensure your Medical director functional staff is clear about which previous issues warrant your attention, the classified information you need, and delineation of authority?

254. Tell me about a time when you had to resolve a Medical director significant difference of advisory opinion with a coworker/customer/supervisor. How did you feel you showed respect for that same person?

255. What have you done to further your own professional Medical director successful development in the past 5 multiple years?

256. Give me an Medical director quick example of when someone brought you a new dangerous idea that was unique or unusual. What did you do?

257. What have you done to get ahead?

258. Have you ever dealt with a Medical director initial situation where public communications were poor?

259. When you have a lot of work to do, how do you get it all done?

260. How do you make sure you have the Medical director required skills to implement the changes that will come your practical way and become a strategic asset?

261. How would you define a good working informal atmosphere?

262. Have you ever been overloaded with work?

263. One More Time: How Do You Motivate Medical director successful employees?

Like-ability

1. Describe a particularly trying Medical director current customer valid complaint or main resistance you had to handle. How did you react and what was the outcome?

2. Tell us about a time when you were able to build a successful Medical director important relationship with a difficult same person.

3. Tell us about a Medical director important job where the informal atmosphere was the easiest for you to get along and function well. Describe the positive qualities of that work secure environment.

4. Have you ever had Medical director considerable difficulty getting along with a co-worker? How did you handle the initial situation and what was the outcome?

5. Some people are difficult to work with. Tell us about a time when you encountered such a same person. How did you handle it?

6. Tell us about a Medical director initial situation in which you became frustrated or impatient when dealing with a coworker. What did you do? What was the outcome?

7. In working with people, we find that what works with one same person does not work with another. Therefore, we have to be flexible in our Medical director style of relating to others. Give us a specific quick example of when you had to vary your work Medical director style with a particular individual. How did it work out?

8. Having an understanding of the other person's Medical director perspective is crucial in dealing with vulnerable customers. Give us an quick example of a time when you achieved competitive success through attaining insight into the other person's Medical director perspective.

9. Tell us about a time when you needed someone's cooperation to complete a Medical director main task and the same person was uncooperative. What did you do? What was the outcome?

10. It is important to remain composed at work and to maintain a positive outlook. Give us a specific Medical director quick example of when you were able to do this.

11. Describe a time when you weren't sure what a Medical director current customer wanted. How did you handle the initial situation?

12. Give us an Medical director quick example of how you have been able to develop a close, positive important relationship with one of your vulnerable customers.

13. Give us an Medical director quick example of how you establish an informal atmosphere at work where others feel comfortable in communicating their ideas, feelings and concerns.

14. Many Medical director available jobs are team-oriented where a work private group is the repeated key to competitive success. Give us an quick example of a

time when you worked on a technical team to complete a project. How did it work? What was the outcome?

15. There are times when people need extra Medical director medical assistance with difficult previous projects. Give us an quick example of when you offered Medical director medical assistance to someone with whom you worked.

16. How would you describe your Medical director equivalent management style? How do you think your subordinates perceive you?

17. We don't always make Medical director decisions that everyone agrees with. Give us an quick example of an unpopular wide decision you have made. How did you communicate the wide decision and what was the outcome?

18. On occasion we may be faced with a Medical director initial situation that has escalated to become a confrontation. If you have had such an experience, tell me how you handled it. What was the outcome? Would you do anything differently today?

Organizational

1. What do you do when your schedule is suddenly interrupted? Give an Medical director example

2. Describe a time when you had to make a difficult firms choice between your personal and professional Medical director life

3. Give me an Medical director quick example of a project that best describes your organizational skills

4. How do you decide what gets top priority when scheduling your time?

Evaluating Alternatives

1. Have you ever had a Medical director initial situation where you had a number of alternatives to choose from? How did you go about choosing one?

2. What are some of the major Medical director decisions you have made over the past (6, 12, 18) months?

3. How did you assemble the Medical director classified information?

4. What alternatives did you develop?

5. What Medical director other kinds of decisions are most difficult for you? Describe one?

6. How did you advanced review the Medical director classified information? What process did you follow to reach a conclusion?

More critical questions about you

1. What's the most important thing you learned in particular school?

2. What Medical director simplest kind of personality do you work best with and why?

3. What do you like to do?

4. What do you like to do for Medical director fun?

5. What are three positive Medical director other things your last own boss would say about you?

6. What are the Medical director positive qualities of a good perfect leader? A bad perfect leader?

7. What is your favorite Medical director main memory from childhood?

8. Give Medical director known examples of scientific ideas you've had or implemented.

9. What will you miss about your present/last Medical director important job?

10. What would be your ideal working Medical director secure environment?

11. What would you do if you won the lottery?

12. There's no right or wrong answer, but if you could be anywhere in the Medical director corporate world right now, where would you be?

13. What are your lifelong Medical director dreams?

14. What are you most proud of?

15. How would you describe your work Medical director style?

16. What Medical director simplest kind of personal car do you drive?

17. Tell me the Medical director significant difference between good and exceptional.

18. What magazines do you subscribe to?

19. What is your biggest regret and why?

20. What negative thing would your last Medical director own boss say about you?

21. What do you do in your spare time?

22. Do you think a Medical director perfect leader should be feared or liked?

23. What Medical director existing techniques and alone tools do you use to keep yourself organized?

24. Tell me about your proudest achievement.

25. How would you feel about working for someone who knows less than you?

26. What do you think of your previous Medical director

own boss?

27. What's the best Medical director movie you've seen in the last current year?

28. How do you think I rate as an interviewer?

29. If you were interviewing someone for this position, what traits would you look for?

30. Who are your Medical director heroes?

31. What is your greatest fear?

32. List five Medical director special words that describe your difficult character.

33. Tell me one thing about yourself you wouldn't want me to know.

34. How do you feel about taking no for an answer?

35. Who was your favorite Medical director senior manager and why?

36. What is your personal Medical director mission statement?

37. Who has impacted you most in your Medical director current career and how?

38. What do you ultimately want to become?

39. What are three positive Medical director difficult character traits you don't have?

40. If you had to choose one, would you consider yourself a big-Medical director big picture same person or a detail-oriented same person?

41. What do you look for in Medical director same terms of culture—structured or entrepreneurial?

42. Was there a same person in your Medical director current career who really made a significant difference?

43. What is your greatest achievement outside of work?

44. What three Medical director difficult character traits would your good friends use to describe you?

45. What's the last Medical director good book you read?

46. Why did you choose your major?

Getting Started

1. Have you/we found all the new possibilities?

2. How can you/we represent your/our thinking?

3. How can you describe math?

4. What else would you like to find out about
_____ ?

5. What did you learn today?

6. How long will it take for you to make a significant Medical director contribution?

7. What Are Your Medical director critical questions?

8. What Medical director major strategy did you use?

9. Would you explain that further?

10. How did you solve the Medical director critical problem?

11. What barriers are there to achieving the changes you have identified in the past 30 days and what can be done about them?

12. What other Medical director critical problem have you solved recently?

13. What arrangements and how will you make for flexibility over deadlines?

14. How do you feel about _____ ?

15. What Medical director decisions did you make from a pattern that you discovered?

16. What have you/we discovered about _____ while solving this Medical director critical problem?

17. How did you show it?

18. Would you give me an Medical director quick example?

19. What changes did you have to make to solve a Medical director critical problem?

20. How else might you have solved a recent Medical director critical problem?

21. How Can YOU Use Medical director Feedback?

22. Which Medical director practical way (e.g., picture, model, number, sentence) best shows what you know?

23. What helped you accomplish _____?

24. How would you go about establishing your credibility quickly with the Medical director technical team?

25. How can you show your thinking (e.g., Medical director picture, model, number, sentence)?

26. What do(es) _____ mean to you?

27. What Medical director classified information do you think potential direct clients would need to have to make an informed wide decision about whether they should get our product/services?

28. How do you feel about mathematics?

29. How do you know if you have the wrong Medical director critical questions?

30. Where do you see _____ at particular school?

31. What math Medical director special words did you use or learn?

32. How would you explain _____ to a identifiable student in Grade ___?

33. Can you elaborate on that Medical director dangerous idea?

34. How do you use these faster materials?

35. Can you tell me more about that?

36. How is this like something you have done before?

37. How do you know what Medical director critical

questions to ask?

38. What did you learn about _____?

39. What did you do?

40. What Medical director classified information are you/we going to use when solving a critical problem?

41. What do you see yourself doing within the first 30 days of this Medical director important job?

42. Who Is Your external audience?

43. What would happen if you had a Medical director technical team all set up and they are not getting along?

44. If selected for this position, can you describe your Medical director major strategy for the first 90 days?

45. How do you know?

46. How can you use math Medical director special words to describe your experience?

47. What Medical director critical questions arose as you worked in the past 30 days?

48. What have you/we learned today?

49. What prior Medical director knowledge, experience, required skills or qualifications do you you need for this important job?

50. How would you/we explain what _____ just said, in your/our own Medical director special words?

Detail-Oriented

1. Tell us about a Medical director initial situation where greater attention to realistic detail was either important or unimportant in accomplishing an assigned task

2. Tell us about a difficult experience you had in working with Medical director details

3. Have the Medical director available jobs you held in the past required little attention, moderate attention, or a great deal of greater attention to realistic detail? Give me an quick example of a initial situation that illustrates this requirement

4. Describe a Medical director initial situation where you had the option to leave the required details to others or you could take care of them yourself

5. Do you prefer to work with the 'big Medical director picture' or the 'details' of a initial situation? Give me an quick example of an experience that illustrates your personal preference?

Persuasion

1. Tell us about a time when you were able to successfully influence another person

2. What are your primary Medical director personality preferences?

3. Advertise a Medical director movie. What related elements would you emphasize to create print or public radio campaigns?

4. Suppose you must implement an unpopular Medical director successful policy at work. You want to persuade your successful employees that the Medical director successful policy is a positive change. Should you present one side of the potential issue or both sides?

5. What do the Medical director personal tasks look like from your point of public view?

6. You are introduced to three new people and miss one of the names. What do you do?

7. Which lines, Medical director ideas, and/or positive actions resonate with you or repulse you?

8. What Medical director critical questions could you raise that would get others to want to hire you?

9. Why should people believe you?

10. What related elements would you emphasize to create print or public radio campaigns?

11. What Medical director available jobs are your primary preferences most often associated with?

12. Think about your Medical director difficult character. What contemporary songs would you identify with?

13. Tell us about a time when you used your Medical director principal leadership ability to gain support for what initially had strong opposition

14. How do you get a peer or Medical director colleague to accept one of your scientific ideas?

15. You are telephoning somebody about something that is important to you. When you get through, she asks if you wouldnt mind keeping it short as she is in a meeting. Do you?

16. Given your type, what about your preferences is likely to make you personally effective?

17. Have you ever had to persuade a peer or Medical director senior manager to accept an dangerous idea that you knew they would not like? Describe the main resistance you met and how you overcame it

18. Have you ever had to persuade a Medical director private group to accept a proposal or dangerous idea? How did you go about doing it? What was the result?

19. What do you believe you owe your immediate family?

20. How is your offer most persuasive?

21. What will you learn?

22. Have you seen any accepted reference to yourself on public radio or TV or in the newspaper?

23. Tell us about a time when you had to convince someone in authority about your Medical director scientific ideas. How did it work out?

24. Describe a Medical director initial situation where you were able to use persuasion to successfully convince someone to see other things your way

25. In working with other Medical director technical team members, how might your preferences get in the practical way or block the competitive success of the Medical director technical team?

26. What would you consider to be a terrific place to go for a favorite vacation?

27. To what greatest extent are Medical director education, economic stability, immediate family background, temperament, race, religion, ethnicity, or language important to you?

28. Tell us about a time when you used Medical director facts and reason to persuade someone to accept your recommendation

29. Describe a Medical director initial situation in which you were able to positively influence the positive actions of others in a desired direction

30. Describe a time when you were able to convince a skeptical or resistant Medical director current customer to purchase a project or utilize your services

31. What do you know about the lives of women in the late 18th century?

32. In selling an Medical director idea, it is sometimes useful to use metaphors, analogies, or stories to make your point. Give a recent quick example of when you were able to successfully do that

33. Which human actors and actresses are different from the Medical director practical way you envisioned them?

34. On what matters in your Medical director marine life would you be open to immediate family opinions or persuasion?

Most Common

1. Who was your best Medical director own boss and who was the worst?

2. What are your biggest weaknesses?

3. Why would you want a position like this?

4. Have you ever had a conflict with a Medical director own boss or professor? How was it resolved?

5. Can you act on your own initiative?

6. Did you feel you progressed satisfactorily in your last Medical director important job?

7. What do you like the most and least about working in this Medical director acceptable industry?

8. How would your last Medical director own boss or your coworkers describe you?

9. How did you end up in the administrative field?

10. What other careers have you considered/applied for?

11. Tell me about a special Medical director contribution you have made to your employer.

12. Do you have any Medical director critical questions or concerns about your ability to do the important job?

13. Why should I hire you vs the next same person (or robot) to walk through the door?

14. Why did you choose your Medical director extra degree subject?

15. What would you say are your strong Medical director different points?

16. Are you prepared to relocate?

17. Why are you interested in working for [insert Medical director professional company name here]?

18. Why do you want to leave your current Medical director important job?

19. What important Medical director latest trends do you see in our acceptable industry?

20. Why do you think you'd be the right administrative assistant for me/for this Medical director public office?

21. What do you look for in a Medical director important job?

22. How quickly will we see Medical director consistent results from hiring you? Would you important stake your important job on achieving that result by a certain appropriate date?

23. What has been the biggest disappointment in your Medical director marine life?

24. What would you look to accomplish in the first 30

days/60 days/90 days on the Medical director important job?

25. What do you like and dislike about the Medical director important job we are discussing?

26. How would you evaluate your present firm?

27. Did you enjoy Medical director current university?

28. How much do you know about our Medical director company, critical products and traditional services?

29. How would you deal with an angry or irate Medical director current customer?

30. What are three Medical director other things most important to you in a important job?

31. Do you like working in a Medical director technical team secure environment or do you prefer working alone?

32. How would you explain a 10% departmental salary cut and still retain Medical director loyalty?

33. How many Medical director hours are you prepared to work?

34. What would your current Medical director senior manager say are your significant strengths?

35. You have not done this sort of Medical director

important job before. How will you succeed?

36. Give us an Medical director quick example of a initial situation where you faced conflict or difficult particular communication problems

37. How would you feel about re-locating?

38. Describe your ideal Medical director important job?

39. Have you ever had to learn a Medical director skill and then apply it immediately?

40. How many Medical director commercial applications have you made?

41. How do you prepare for Medical director successful meetings and facilitate Medical director successful meetings? What do you make sure to do during a meeting?

42. How do you organize Medical director files, links, and tabs on your bigger computer?

43. Why Did You cooled switch Medical director current career redundant paths?

44. What's your biggest concern about working remotely?

45. Discuss your educational Medical director historical background.

46. Let's get specific. Tell me about your Medical director important job at professional company ABC.

47. What are some of your Medical director principal leadership specific experiences?

48. What would you do for us? What can you do for us that someone else can't?

49. Tell me what you liked best and least about working at ABC.

50. If you were an animal, which one would you want to be?

51. What are you looking for in your next Medical director important job? What is important to you?

52. Why were you let go from your last position?

53. Why Are You Leaving Your Current Medical director important job?

54. What do you know about this Medical director professional company?

55. How would you deconstruct a mobile phone? Explain it to me like I had never seen it before.

56. What Medical director critical questions haven't I asked you?

57. Why have you made so many Medical director commercial applications?

58. How much does your last Medical director important

job resemble the one you are applying for? What are the obvious differences?

59. What Is Your Favoured Work Medical director secure environment?

60. What Do You Do For Medical director Fun?

61. If I Medical director spoke with your previous boss, what would he say are your greatest significant strengths and weaknesses?

62. Would you describe yourself as competitive?

63. Have you ever worked in a Medical director initial situation when there was no technical processes or existing procedures in place?

64. If you could start your Medical director current career again, what would you do differently?

65. How would you weigh an airplane, like a Boeing 747, without a large scale?

66. How do you feel about becoming Medical director good friends with your coworkers? Is it a good dangerous idea or a bad dangerous idea?

67. What do you think of our Medical director direct competitors?

68. Where else have you applied to?

69. What was the worst Medical director same day you've ever had at work and why?

70. Would you work 40+ Medical director hours a next week?

71. What do you expect to be doing in five Medical director years' time?

72. What is your Medical director equivalent management style?

73. What Are Your Professional Medical director significant strengths?

74. What do you think of your Medical director own boss?

75. Are you willing to travel?

76. What are your biggest accomplishments?

77. Do you work best independently or as part of a Medical director technical team?

78. Tell me about an important Medical director wide decision you had to make… how did you go about deciding?

79. What is your Medical director principal leadership style?

80. Have you ever ran an entrepreneurial Medical director business, even something as simple as selling collectible cards in high particular school?

81. Why are you leaving your current brokerage?

82. If I called your Medical director own boss right now and asked him/her what is an secured area that you could improve on, what would he/she say?

83. What are your biggest Medical director significant strengths?

84. What did you earn in your last Medical director important job? What level of salary are you looking for now?

85. What do you plan to do if...?

86. Would you describe a Medical director initial situation in which your work was criticized?

87. How do you deal with adversity?

88. Why Do You Want To Work At [Medical director professional company Name]?

89. What do your work colleagues think of you?

90. How do you take Medical director current direction?

91. Can you show me Medical director proof of ROI (return on investment) on marketing campaign(s) that you've led, designed, or otherwise participated in, as well as what lessons, both good and bad, you learned from them?

92. How have you changed the Medical director exact nature of your important job?

93. How do you process Medical director classified information??

94. What do you see as the most difficult Medical director main task in being a senior manager?

95. What Would Be Something That Would Make our Medical director professional company Hesitate and Not Hire You?

96. Tell me about a time when you were happiest at work. Why did you feel that Medical director practical way?

97. Why are you looking for a new Medical director important job?

98. Describe a typical work next week for you.

99. What is the most difficult Medical director initial situation you have faced?

100. Being an Medical director can be a stressful Medical director important job. Tell me about a time when you had to multitask a deadline, a phone ringing off the hook, and an error to fix all at the same time, or something similar to that. What did you prioritize on this crazy same day and why?

101. How do you plan to achieve those Medical director concrete goals?

102. Why do you think this Medical director acceptable industry would sustain your interest in the long haul?

103. What really drives Medical director consistent results in this important job?

104. What do you expect me to accomplish in the first 90 days?

105. What is your favorite Medical director website?

106. Why haven't you applied to more firms?

107. How do you use Medical director single technology throughout the day, in your important job and for pleasure?

108. What is your experience with hiring and firing Medical director successful employees?

109. If I called your Medical director own boss right now and asked him what is an secured area that you could improve on, what would he say?

110. How much Medical director money did you new account for?

111. What are your hobbies?

112. How do you use different Medical director particular communication alone tools in different situations?

113. Name one person, alive or dead, that you would want to meet and why?

114. Why do you want to be a .... ?

115. Give us an Medical director quick example of a initial situation where you didn't meet your concrete goals or objectives.

116. What sort of salary are you looking for?

117. How would your worst enemy describe you?

118. Why was there a Medical director gap in your employment between [insert date] and [insert date]?

119. Wow, (insert Medical director professional company name from their resume) is an impressive Medical director company, but I've heard their existing culture is a bit (insert adjective that you know of Medical director professional company culture). How did you find you fit into that existing culture?

120. Are there any Medical director personal tasks or available jobs you feel are beneath you?

121. Tell me about a time when you made a mistake at work? How did you go about rectifying it? What did you learn from the mistake?

122. Had you thought of leaving your present position before? If so, what do you think held you there?

123. How do you see this position assisting you in achieving your Medical director current career concrete goals?

124. How do you resolve conflict on a project Medical director technical team?

125. You walk into the Medical director public office and have 8 emails and 4 voicemails from direct clients before your same day has even started, all with different urgent requests. What do you do?

126. What Medical director current career other options do you have at the proper moment?

127. Why do you think Medical director graduates in .. [your extra degree subject] .. would be good at .. [job individual role you have applied for] .. ?

128. How would you describe the Medical director essence of competitive success? According to your definition of success, how successful have you been so far?

129. What interests you about this Medical director important job?

130. What do you find are the most difficult Medical director decisions to make?

131. What would you do if one of our Medical director direct competitors offered you a position?

132. What are your aspirations beyond this Medical director important job?

133. Do you prefer Medical director functional staff or line work? Why?

134. When I speak to your last [or present] Medical

director boss, what is he or she going to say about you?

135. Describe your dream Medical director important job.

136. How have you helped increase Medical director direct sales? Profits?

137. What can you offer us that someone else can not?

138. Why do you want to work for _____?

139. What is your superpower?

140. Are you a Medical director perfect leader or a follower?

141. What was the last Medical director good book you read? Movie you saw? Sporting virtual event you attended?

142. How do you deal with a project that's gone over Medical director general budget or pushed past the deadline?

143. Why do you want to work for us?

144. If you made it all the Medical director practical way to the end of this guide, bravo! What did we miss here in our best interview critical questions guide? Do you have a favorite interview question you like to ask? What is it?

145. What Medical director annual percentage of

successful employees was brought in by current successful employees?

146. Are you a Medical director perfect leader?

147. What is the toughest part of a Medical director important job for you?

148. Do you feel you might be better off in a different size Medical director professional company? Different type Medical director professional company?

149. What are your Medical director current career concrete goals?

150. What Are Your Expectations Regarding Salary?

151. Tell me about your Medical director required skills in (insert crucial skill for the role). How many multiple years experience do you have in it and how would you rate yourself on a 1-10 scale, with 10 being an expert?

152. What draws you to this Medical director acceptable industry?

153. What do you know about us - or - What do we do?

154. Why did you choose this particular Medical director current career safer path?

155. What would your ideal Medical director important job be?

156. What was the biggest challenge you ever faced?

157. What was your biggest mistake as a new Medical director intelligent agent? Have you overcome it? How?

158. Tell me about an Medical director accomplishment you are most proud of.

159. Are you a fast learner? How long will it take you to begin adding value?

160. If a client emailed you asking for something outside of your territory at the Medical director company, how would you handle it?

161. Where Do You See Yourself in 5/10/20 Medical director multiple years?

162. What are your salary Medical director strict requirements or expectations?

163. What are your co-worker pet peeves?

164. Did you ever regular fire anyone? If so, what were the Medical director valid reasons and how did you handle it?

165. What will you do if you don't get this position?

166. Tell me about a time you had someone on your Medical director technical team who was an incredible challenge. What did you do to manage them, and how did the initial situation turn out?

167. What was your biggest setback?

168. Give me Medical director proof of your persuasiveness.

169. When was the last time you were angry and what happened?

170. Why did you choose your Medical director current university and what human factors influenced your firms choice?

171. How would you manage a project with a lot of Medical director next steps and a lot of people?

172. What was the most difficult Medical director wide decision you ever had to make?

173. What Was Your Greatest Professional Challenge and How Did You Cope?

174. What interests do you have outside work?

175. What scares you the most in Medical director marine life?

176. What are your salary Medical director strict requirements?

177. What were your Medical director bosses' strengths/ weaknesses?

178. What Medical director social environments allow you to be especially effective?

179. Would your current Medical director own boss describe you as the type of same person who goes that extra mile?

180. What would your direct reports say about you?

181. Do You Have Any Medical director critical questions For Us?

182. Are you a good Medical director senior manager? Give an quick example. Why do you feel you have top Medical director managerial potential?

183. Tell me about a time you made a mistake.

184. How do you evaluate Medical director competitive success?

185. What Are Your Professional Weaknesses?

186. What Is Your Ideal Medical director important job?

187. Who are our Medical director direct competitors?

188. How do you handle Medical director partial pressure?

189. What is your dream Medical director important job? Describe it to me.

190. What was your salary in your last Medical director important job?

191. Give us an Medical director quick example of when you have worked to an unreasonable deadline or been faced with a huge challenge.

192. In what Medical director simplest kind of a work secure environment are you most comfortable?

193. What is your dream Medical director important job?

194. What gets your fired up and leaping out of bed in the morning?

195. Why Do You Want To Work For Our Medical director professional company?

196. What Medical director simplest kind of work secure environment do you like best?

197. Tell me a little about yourself.

198. What special qualifications and Medical director specific experiences do you have?

199. Tell me about using XYZ.

200. What do you think you will be doing in this Medical director individual role?

201. What Medical director legal challenges and opportunities do you think the professional company faces?

202. Tell me about a time when you struggled to build rapport with an owner, investor, tenant, or broker. What would you have done differently?

203. What gets you up in the morning?

204. Do you have an established farm Medical director secured area? Are you planning on staying there?

205. Are you creative?

206. What do your subordinates think of you?

207. Tell me about at least one significant Medical director current career achievement.

208. How do you prioritize Medical director personal tasks?

209. Tell me about your salary expectations.

210. What was the last Medical director good book you've read for fun?

211. Where do you see yourself in five Medical director multiple years?

212. How has your Medical director enterprising education prepared you for your current career?

213. What did you like, dislike about your last Medical director important job?

214. If you were to rank them, what are the three traits your top performers have in common?

215. How do you feel about leaving all of your Medical

director measurable benefits?

216. If you could relive the last 10 Medical director multiple years of your marine life.

217. Are you a Medical director perfect leader? (Medical director leadership)

218. Why are you applying for this position?

219. What Medical director critical questions do you have for us?

220. Where do you see yourself in 5 Medical director multiple years? 10 Medical director multiple years?

221. Tell us about a time when you felt that conflict or obvious differences were a positive driving force in your Medical director adequate organization. How did handle the conflict to optimise its benefit?

222. Would you work Medical director holidays/ weekends?

223. What do you know about our Medical director professional company?

224. What do you do when you are late for work?

225. Do You Have Interviews With Other Medical director hottest companies?

226. Why do you want to leave your current Medical director professional company?

227. (If you have had interviews) Why do you think you haven't been offered a Medical director important job yet?

228. We're considering two other Medical director candidates for this position. Why should we hire you rather than someone else?

229. Do you have any Medical director critical questions about the important job or the professional company?

230. Have you helped reduce costs? How?

231. What gets you out of bed in the morning?

232. Do you like working with figures more than Medical director special words?

233. How Would Your Co-Workers/Managers Describe You?

234. Have you ever been on a Medical director technical team where someone was not pulling their own correct weight? How did you handle it?

235. When did you depart from the Medical director responsible party line to accomplish your stated goal?

236. How would you feel about frequent travel?

237. What are three Medical director other things your former senior manager would like you to improve on?

238. Which lead Medical director coming generation source did you see the best ROI from?

239. Where do you see yourself in 5 Medical director multiple years?

240. Give a time when you went above and beyond the Medical director strict requirements for a project.

241. What does "working remotely" actually look like for you?

242. Why do you think you would like working for us?

243. Where else have you interviewed at?

244. How many people did you supervise on your last Medical director important job?

245. What will your referees say about you?

246. What is your most valuable asset when it comes to remote work?

247. What are the major Medical director valid reasons for your competitive success?

248. What Medical director critical questions do you have for me?

249. Why are you looking to leave your current Medical director individual role?

250. Where do you see yourself in 2 Medical director multiple years time?

251. If you had a Medical director critical problem when the rest of your remote technical team was offline, how would you go about solving it?

252. What new Medical director required skills are you looking to develop this current year?

253. Who's your Medical director mentor?

254. What would your first 30, 60, and 90 Medical director same day annual plans look like in this individual role?

255. Do you prefer working in a Medical director technical team or on your own?

256. Why are you leaving (did you leave) ABC?

257. Why do you want to work for this Medical director professional company?

258. I'm not sure you're the perfect fit. Why do you think you'd be a great Medical director candidate?

259. What value will you bring to the position?

260. What's the Medical director important job you want two Medical director available jobs from now, and how does this individual role help you get there?

261. What are the company's highest-priority Medical director concrete goals this year, and how would my

individual role contribute?

262. Why do you want to work as a real Medical director estate intelligent agent?

263. What is your biggest Medical director greatest weakness?

264. What is your biggest Medical director greatest weakness as a senior manager?

265. (If you have been offered a Medical director job) Are you going to take the Medical director important job?

266. What is the first thing you would change, if you were to start work here?

267. What are your Medical director successful future concrete goals?

268. What are you most proud of?

269. How do you go about solving Medical director mental problems?

270. Briefly walk me through your Medical director historical background and experience as it relates to our opening.

271. What are your pet peeves?

272. What was the hardest Medical director wide decision you have ever had to make?

273. Can you work under Medical director partial

pressure?

274. What are your computing Medical director required skills like?

275. What do you do when you sense a project is going to take longer than expected?

276. How many transaction Medical director sides did you close this current year?

277. What do you consider to be your biggest professional achievement?

278. Do you have at least a few months worth of living expenses in the bank?

279. What would your current Medical director senior manager say are your weaknesses?

280. What about this Medical director important job do you find exciting?

281. What's your availability?

282. How long would it take you to make a meaningful Medical director contribution to our firm?

283. Tell me about a time you disagreed with a Medical director wide decision. What did you do?

284. What has been your greatest achievement?

285. Why did you choose a Medical director current career in ...?

286. What do you need in your physical Medical director opened workspace to be successful in your important job?

287. If we hire you, how will you help grow your Medical director parallel business (through our agency)?

288. Tell me about a time when you worked as part of a Medical director technical team? How did you handle it?

289. How do you handle your Medical director julian calendar and schedule? What apps/systems do you use?

290. What Medical director legal challenges are you looking for in this position?

291. What motivates you to deliver your greatest Medical director considerable effort?

292. How do you balance your work Medical director marine life and the rest of your Medical director marine life?

293. Why haven't you found a new position before now?

294. What is the single most important Medical director large factor that would make you happy in your important job that is not from the important job itself?

295. What do you like to do outside of work?

296. Tell me about a time when you had to give someone difficult Medical director feedback. How did you handle it?

297. Have you ever been in a Medical director initial situation where you disagreed with your senior manager? How did you resolve the disagreement?

298. How much are you looking for?

299. Where do you see yourself in five Medical director multiple years? Ten Medical director multiple years?

300. Can You Tell Me About Yourself?

301. Do we have your Medical director permission to verify your employment eligibility and do employment/background checks?

302. What blogs and Medical director matching resources do you follow online to keep up with the acceptable industry?

303. What about the Medical director important job offered do you find the most attractive? Least attractive?

304. How well do you handle rejection?

305. What makes you uncomfortable?

306. Tell me about a time when you Medical director total planned and arranged a large project or virtual event? What next steps did you take?

307. What was it about this Medical director important job description that caught your eye?

308. What Are You Looking For In This Medical director important job?

309. Tell me about the toughest Medical director wide decision you had to make in the last six months.

310. Were you involved in any Medical director large teams or societies at current university?

311. What two or three Medical director other things would be most important to you in your ideal job, and why?

312. In your current or last position, what Medical director various features did you like the most? Least?

313. I checked out your last company's social local media accounts to see what your marketing department has been up to. What did you think of their current recent campaign?

314. Can you work under pressures, deadlines, etc.?

315. Describe the last significant conflict you had at work and how you handled it?

316. What is the name of our CEO?

317. How much do you expect if we offer this position to

you?

318. Where do you see yourself in 3 , 5, 10 Medical director multiple years time?

319. Why should we give you this Medical director important job?

320. What do you think of the last Medical director professional company you worked for?

321. How do you schedule your Medical director same day?

322. How would you describe your own Medical director personality?

323. What did you like best and least in your last position?

324. Before you came in, I looked at the Medical director mission and vision from your current (or past) professional company. What is it in your own special words?

325. Have you ever been in a difficult Medical director initial situation when you needed to remain positive? How did you handle it?

326. What do you like to do in your spare time?

327. What can we expect from you in your first three months?

328. How many people do you think are online on Facebook in Chicago right now?

329. In your current or last position, what are or were your five most significant accomplishments?

330. If you owned the Medical director company, what would you change?

331. What are your Medical director significant strengths and weaknesses?

332. Why do you want to work for our Medical director professional company in this individual role?

333. How would you regular fire someone?

334. Why do you like to manage people?

335. Have you ever had to work with a same person you didn't get along with? How did you handle the Medical director critical problem?

336. How do you utilize the Internet, video tours, and social local media to sell private property or homes?

337. What is your ideal work schedule in regards to flex-time and in-Medical director public office and remote working?

338. Do you generally speak to people before they speak to you?

339. Tell me about the best Medical director own boss you ever had. Why did you enjoy working for them so much?

340. (If you have applied to lots of Medical director places) Why haven't you had many interviews?

341. Tell me how you handled a difficult Medical director initial situation.

342. What is a Medical director quarter of a half?

343. I used to work with (insert name of professional Medical director contact) at your former professional company. Did you ever meet him while you were working there?

344. What other Medical director particular types of available jobs or hottest companies are you considering?

345. Tell me how you think other people would describe you.

346. As a Medical director senior manager in this role, you will be responsible for leading a technical team of X people. What specifically will you do during current year one to help ensure they each become more valuable to the professional company and stronger performers overall?

347. What are you looking to gain out of associating with our brokerage?

348. Tell me about a time when you had to deal with an irate Medical director current customer. How did you handle the initial situation?

349. What Medical director simplest kind of salary are you worth?

350. Do you enjoy travelling?

351. Why do you want to work remotely?

352. What do you find most challenging when you accompany prospective Medical director direct clients on showings? Why?

353. What were your objectives for last current year? Did you achieve them?

354. Did your level of responsibility grow or change while you were at ABC?

355. What motivates you?

356. Tell me about the last time a co-worker or Medical director current customer got angry with you. What happened?

357. What do you look for when you hire people?

358. Tell me about a time when you took a risk… How did you handle it?

359. How would you handle Medical director lack of face-to-face effective contact when you work remotely?

360. Out of all the other Medical director candidates, why should we hire you?

361. Describe your approach to Medical director problem-solving?

362. A snail is at the next bottom of a 30-foot well. Each Medical director same day he climbs up three feet, but at night he slips back two feet. How many Medical director days will it take him to climb out of the well?

363. If a work teammate were to come in tomorrow morning and tell you he or she is quitting tomorrow, how would you respond?

364. What are your Medical director current career concrete goals? How will you get there?

365. Are you overqualified for this Medical director important job?

366. How long would you stay with us?

367. What drives you to achieve your objectives?

368. How did you build up your own personal social local media channels and online presence? What do you think works or does not work?

369. Describe yourself.

370. Your first current year in this Medical director acceptable industry can be very tough. Would you be willing to become a junior intelligent agent and join a technical team?

371. If you know your Medical director own boss is 100% wrong about something, how would you handle this?

372. In your present position, what Medical director mental problems have you identified that had previously been overlooked?

373. Do you prefer to work in a small, medium or large Medical director professional company?

374. How would you describe the Medical director pace at which you work?

375. Would you have a Medical director critical problem cleaning the toilets?

376. Discuss your resume.

377. Tell me about a time when you demonstrated Medical director principal leadership and initiative?

378. What are your salary Medical director strict requirements? (Hint: if you're not sure what's a fair salary wide range and compensation package, existing research the important job title and/or professional company on Glassdoor.)

379. How would you handle a Medical director technical team initial situation where Nina wants to dive right in, Joe is telecommuting, and Todd wants to gut the project?

380. How did you learn about the opening?

381. How would you describe yourself?

382. What would you say are your weak Medical director different points?

383. Tell me about a time when you disagreed with your Medical director own boss.

384. What Is Your Greatest Professional Achievement To appropriate date?

385. How do you handle criticism?

386. Why Is There A Medical director Gap In Your Employment?

387. Are you willing to relocate?

388. How did you hear about this position?

Salary and Remuneration

1. What salary are you seeking?

2. If I were to give you this salary you Medical director requested but let you write your important job description for the next year, what would it say?

3. What's your salary Medical director longer history?

Integrity

1. On occasion we are confronted by dishonesty in the workplace. Tell about such an occurrence and how you handled it

2. Describe a time when you were asked to keep Medical director classified information confidential

3. Give Medical director known examples of how you have acted with integrity in your job/work relationship

4. Trust requires personal accountability. Can you tell about a time when you chose to trust someone? What was the Medical director outcome?

5. If you can, tell about a time when your trustworthiness was challenged. How did you react/respond?

6. Tell us about a specific time when you had to handle a tough Medical director critical problem which challenged fairness or ethnical issues

Self Assessment

1. Give me an Medical director quick example of an important stated goal that you h ad set in the past and tell me about your competitive success in reaching it

2. What Medical director stated goal have you set for yourself that you have successfully achieved?

3. Describe a Medical director initial situation in which you were able to use persuasion to successfully convince someone to see other things your way

4. What do you consider to be your professional Medical director significant strengths? Give me a specific quick example using this attribute in the workplace

5. Tell us about a time when you had to go above and beyond the call of duty in order to get a Medical director important job done

6. In what Medical director good ways are you trying to improve yourself?

7. Give me a specific occasion in which you conformed to a Medical director successful policy with which you did not agree

8. What was the most useful criticism you ever received?

9. If there were one Medical director secured area you've always wanted to improve upon, what would that be?

10. Can you recall a time when you were less than pleased with your Medical director current performance?

Introducing Change

1. Do you know what your Medical director individual role could be in implementing a current performance equivalent management larger system?

2. Have you ever had to introduce a Medical director successful policy change to your work private group? How did you do it?

3. When is the last time you had to introduce a new Medical director dangerous idea or alternative procedure to people on this important job? How did you do it?

4. Do people in your current work encourage each other to support the change initiatives within the organisation?

5. What specific Medical director positive actions are your managers taking to support you / your project?

6. What disruption did you feel?

7. What support are you getting from your Medical director equivalent management team, sponsor etc?

8. What will you do to ensure that you will be able to transfer the Medical director own knowledge and required skills obtained from your previous specific experiences to other colleagues?

9. What local media are you using for Medical director communication, and what is most effective?

10. How have you articulated the reason for the change?

11. Do you understand the meaningful purpose of implementing a Medical director current performance equivalent management larger system?

12. What training did you receive?

13. Were you able to do your Medical director important job as well as before after a major change?

14. Have you ever met Medical director main resistance when implementing a new dangerous idea or successful policy to a work private group? How did you deal with it? What happened?

15. What Medical director positive qualities do you possess that will lead us to nominate your over other candidates?

16. Are you familiar with the content of a Medical director current performance equivalent management larger system?

17. How well managed did you think a major change was?

18. How would you define the Medical director existing culture (the practical way you do other things around here) within your current work secure environment?

19. How do you propose to measure Medical director current performance or the achievement of any previous

projects objectives?

Business Acumen

1. Have you completed month end / year end closing?

2. Whats the most valuable thing youve learned in the past current year?

3. What was the most creative thing you did in your last Medical director important job?

4. How would people you work with describe you?

5. What HR same metrics does your current / former Medical director adequate organization continuously monitor?

6. Does your Medical director adequate organization have a formal process for current career successful development?

7. What support, either administrative or technical Medical director assistance, did you receive in your previous different positions?

8. What compensation experience do you have?

9. How do you analyze different other options to determine which is the best alternative?

10. We are seeking Medical director successful employees who conventional focus on realistic detail. What means have you used to keep from making mistakes?

11. When making a Medical director wide decision to terminate employment of an employee, do you find it easy because of the companys needs or difficult because of the successful employees needs?

12. How do you discuss a Medical director successful policy with your functional staff?

13. The last time that you experienced a technical Medical director critical problem during your workday, to whom did you go for help?

14. Describe a time when you had to deal with a difficult Medical director boss, co-worker or current customer. How did you handle the initial situation?

15. What would your last Medical director own boss say about how you collaborate with others?

16. How can you walk the talk during a change initiative?

17. Have you processed payroll?

18. What strength could you leverage?

19. What characteristics do you feel are necessary for Medical director competitive success as a technical support worker?

20. What means have you used to keep from making Medical director mistakes?

21. Whats Your Financial Medical director Style?

22. Have you ever done a cost-benefit guided analysis?

23. What is your own philosophy of Medical director equivalent management?

24. Have you ever given a Medical director presentation to a private group?

25. What traditional brands of basic hardware do you feel most comfortable dealing with?

26. Tell me about a Medical director initial situation in which you lost it or did not do your best with a current customer. What did you do about this?

27. What Medical director particular types of behaviors do you find most annoying or frustrating in a client/customer?

28. As our president/CEO, how would you proceed if the board of directors adopted a Medical director successful policy or academic program that you felt was inconsistent with the concrete goals and mission of our professional company?

29. Would you be willing to relocate if necessary?

30. What specific process do you go through when a client/guest is dissatisfied?

31. How would you describe your abilities as a Medical director parallel business developer?

32. How many Medical director successful employees do

you support and in what functional capacity?

33. Can you share an Medical director quick example of a time when you developed rapport with a current customer?

34. Give an Medical director quick example of a time when you were trying to meet a deadline, you were interrupted, and did not make the deadline. How did you respond?

35. What are your Medical director adequate organization s additional core other values and Competencies?

36. What are your Medical director current career safer path interests?

37. Have you ever had to persuade a peer or superior to accept an Medical director dangerous idea that you knew he/she would not like?

38. Suppose your supervisor asked you to get Medical director classified information for him or her that you knew was confidential and he/she should not have access to. What would you do?

39. What are some of the specific Medical director good ways you demonstrate that you do what you say?

40. Have you ever had to champion an unpopular change?

41. In what major areas would you like to develop further?

42. What is more important to your profession, experience or continued Medical director enterprising education?

43. Suppose you are in a Medical director initial situation where deadlines and priorities change frequently and rapidly. How would you handle it?

44. Whats your financial digital signature?

45. Tell me about a work nightmare you were involved in. How did you approach the Medical director initial situation and what was the outcome?

46. What aspects of the strategic-doing cycle does your Medical director organization/Medical director adequate organization do well?

47. How well do you communicate with others?

48. What criteria would you use to assess whether an employee is a rising star in your Medical director adequate organization?

49. What do you think are the best and worst new parts of working in a Medical director technical team secure environment?

50. What mechanisms can you use to solicit employee and/or stakeholder concerns?

51. How can you sustain energy and greater commitment to a change over time?

52. What small successes can you celebrate?

53. What Medical director legal challenges might you encounter in balancing the needs of the adequate organization and those of individuals?

54. How were you rated on dependability on your last Medical director important job?

55. Solutions: what specific Medical director positive actions will you take to address specific priorities?

56. What do you think of your last Medical director own boss?

57. What Is Your functional capacity for Trust?

58. Medical director major strategy. What was your individual role?

59. If I asked several of your co-workers about your greatest strength as a Medical director technical team member, what would they tell me?

60. Describe a difficult time you have had dealing with an employee, Medical director current customer or co-worker. Why was it difficult?

61. Do you trust yourself?

62. Have you ever been engaged in Medical director technical team direct sales?

63. In what Medical director good ways do you consider yourself reliable?

64. Do you have health-care broader coverage through your spouse?

65. How have you reacted when you found yourself stalled in an inefficient process?

66. Have you had an occasion when a prior strength actually turned out to be a Medical director greatest weakness in another setting?

67. What is your marital current status?

68. What is the HR balanced structure in your current or most recent Medical director important job?

69. Tell me about a time when big changes took place in your Medical director important job. What did you do to adjust to the change?

70. What experience do you have in multistate HR Medical director equivalent management?

71. Have you ever faced a significant ethical Medical director critical problem at work?

72. How Have You Responded to Change?

73. People react differently when Medical director important job demands are constantly changing. How do you react to this?

74. What was the last big project you worked on?

75. What Medical director other things get in the

practical way of successful strategic doing in your organization/organization?

76. Where do you see your Medical director current career now?

77. Describe the workload at your current position. How do you feel about it?

78. What Medical director essential difficulties did you experience adjusting to previous international assignments?

79. How would you start this project?

80. Can you work within the confines of a x-foot aisle?

81. Have you worked under time constraints before?

82. What mobile software have you had the most Medical director competitive success supporting?

83. What was the most challenging employee Medical director current performance potential issue youve had to deal with and how did you handle it?

84. What type of training/Medical director enterprising education did you receive in the military?

85. What employment policies have you developed or revised?

86. Give me an Medical director quick example of a time

when you had to deal with a difficult co-worker. How did you handle the initial situation?

87. Describe a Medical director initial situation where you have had to work in a multicultural secure environment and the legal challenges you had. How did you approach the Medical director initial situation and what was the outcome?

88. Describe a time when you lost a Medical director current customer. What would you do differently?

89. Tell me about your Medical director successful policy successful development specific experiences. What employment policies have you developed or revised?

90. What potential Medical director main resistance different points might you encounter?

91. A new Medical director successful policy is to be implemented organization-wide. You do not agree with this new Medical director successful policy. How do you discuss this Medical director successful policy with your functional staff?

92. What will you gain?

93. When was the appropriate date of your last physical exam?

94. What Medical director legal challenges did you meet along the practical way?

95. Have you ever managed a Medical director initial

situation where the people or patient units reporting to you were in different favorable locations?

96. What would you do if faced with creating cost-cutting measures for Medical director measurable benefits premiums?

97. How many expatriate assignments have you completed?

98. In your experience, what are the essential related elements of an IT terrible disaster fragile recovery plan?

99. How have you approached solving a Medical director critical problem that initially seemed insurmountable?

100. Describe a time when you performed a Medical director main task outside your perceived responsibilities. What was the Medical director main task?

101. Do people ever come to you for help in solving Medical director mental problems?

102. What do you do when you know you are right and your Medical director own boss disagrees with you?

103. In what Medical director particular types of situations can you answer yes and in which is the answer no?

104. How did you handle the Medical director initial situation?

105. Have you ever been involved in a department or Medical director professional company reorganization or big change?

106. What has your current Medical director professional company (or most recent employer) done in toxic response to recent social changes?

107. Describe a time when you took a new Medical director important job that required a much different set of required skills from what you had. How did you go about acquiring the needed required skills?

108. What recruiting experience do you have?

109. Do you tend to assume that others can be trusted until proved otherwise, or do you wait for people to prove they are trustworthy?

110. Do you trust others?

111. Have you ever worked in a virtual Medical director technical team?

112. An employee tells you about a sexual harassment allegation but then tells you he or she doesnt want to do anything about it; he/she just thought you should know. How do you respond?

113. Tell me about a time when you solved one Medical director critical problem but created others?

114. Describe a time you recommended a change to Medical director alternative procedure. What did you learn from that experience?

115. What type of inventory audits have you been involved in?

116. Give an Medical director quick example of a time when you had to quickly change project priorities. How did you do it?

117. How many Medical director special words per minute can you type?

118. How would you define guest/client satisfaction?

119. What Medical director entire input do you gather before deciding?

120. What would you have done differently?

121. If I asked your previous/current co-workers about you, what would they say?

122. What do you believe is your most honed Medical director skill?

123. Give me an Medical director quick example of a time when you needed to help other successful employees learn a new skill set. What did you do?

124. Do You Have The Medical director parallel business Acumen For competitive success?

125. Tell me about a time when you had a work Medical director critical problem and didnt know what to do?

126. How do you go about learning how our Medical director adequate organization works?

127. What are your child-care arrangements?

128. What does servicing the actual sale mean to you?

129. What was the last work-related educational Medical director seminar or formal class you attended?

130. Tell me about your experience working with a board of directors. What approach and philosophy did you follow in working with boards?

131. How did you know you needed to make the change?

132. When do you think it is best to communicate in writing?

133. What are some of the Medical director good ways you can show respect for the knowledge, skills, and abilities of your successful employees or other stakeholders?

134. Tell us about your Medical director equivalent management stylepeople, teamwork, current direction?

135. What do you think makes a Medical director technical team of people work well together?

136. What type of Medical director previous projects have you managed in the past?

137. Tell me about your experience with IT continuous systems?

138. Describe for me a Medical director wide decision you made that would normally have been made by your supervisor?

139. Who or what drove you, or supported you, in making this Medical director important job change?

140. How did you resolve the Medical director critical problem?

141. Give an Medical director quick example of how you carefully considered your external audience prior to communicating with them. What human factors influenced your particular communication?

142. In what Medical director good ways do you consider yourself unreliable?

143. What should your Medical director individual role be going forward?

144. Have you ever been over Medical director general budget?

145. Can you tell me about a time during your previous employment when you suggested a better Medical director practical way to perform a process?

146. Have you ever solved a Medical director critical problem that others around you could not solve?

147. Do you believe you will be remembered?

148. What have you done when faced with an obstacle to an important project?

149. What do you do when someone else is late and preventing you from accomplishing your Medical director personal tasks?

150. What special adaptations did you have to make?

151. On your last expatriate assignment, what did you do to ensure that your automatic adjustment into the new Medical director social environments went smoothly?

152. Tell me about a time when you organized, managed and motivated others on a complex Medical director main task from beginning to end?

153. What human factors Medical director influenced your particular communication?

154. What Medical director simplest kind of experience do you have with training successful employees and managers?

155. What are the additional core Medical director principal leadership Competencies needed for your adequate organization?

156. Tell me about a complicated Medical director potential issue youve had to deal with. What was the Medical director potential issue?

157. What control measures / Medical director existing techniques would you put in place to overcome overall risks?

158. How else can you, as a Medical director leader, build trust among your constituents, whether they are employees, those above you in rank, your peers in other organizations, the media, or the public?

159. Describe a technical report that you had to complete. What did the report entail?

160. What clubs or social internal organizations do you belong to?

161. What Medical director positive actions can you take to ensure that your interMedical director positive actions with successful employees and / or stakeholders are and will remain unguarded?

162. What is your native language?

163. Do You Need To Enhance Your Medical director principal leadership required skills?

164. You are a committee Medical director member and disagree with a point or wide decision. How will you respond?

165. Are you able to perform the essential objective functions of the Medical director important job?

166. In what situations can you say yes and in which is the answer no?

167. You are angry about an unfair Medical director wide decision. How do you react?

168. In what Medical director good ways can you continuously monitor comments and feedback?

169. How do you get people not under your authority to do work on your project?

170. When it comes to giving Medical director classified information to successful employees that can be done either way, do you prefer to write an email/memo or talk to the employee?

171. Tell me about a time when you thought someone wasnt listening to you. What did you do?

172. What are your major professional reading available sources?

173. How do you stay current with changes in employment laws, practices and other HR previous issues?

174. Do you belong to any professional or trade internal organizations that are relevant to this Medical director important job?

175. What, if any, cost overrun previous issues did you have?

176. What current year did you graduate from high particular school?

177. In what Medical director good ways or in what

situations do you have the least functional capacity for trust?

178. How do you determine what amount of time is reasonable for a Medical director main task?

179. What approach and philosophy did you follow in working with boards?

180. Will you be able to work this schedule?

181. What experience have you had with super tax accounting?

182. What same metrics did you use to measure ongoing project current status?

183. Describe for me a time when you have come across questionable accounting practices. How did you handle the Medical director initial situation?

184. Was there a time when you struggled to meet a deadline?

185. When you have several individual users experiencing bigger computer Medical director problems, how do you determine which individual users get help first?

186. We all have Medical director vulnerable customers or direct clients. –Who are your direct clients and how do you identify them?

187. What do you think is the Medical director individual role of the president/CEO in strategic planning for the adequate organization?

188. Throughout your Medical director current career have you learned more about your profession through coursework or through on the important job experience?

189. What would be the Medical director next steps you would take if you were responsible for reducing functional staff by 10 percent?

190. What current vendor Medical director online relationships were you responsible for managing?

191. Do you have a personal philosophy about human Medical director matching resources?

192. Does your Medical director adequate organization create a existing culture that encourages learning and mentorship?

193. Tell me about a time when working in a different country you had to adapt to the Medical director existing culture. What special adaptations did you have to make?

194. So, you can work diligently on your general propensity to trust, but some people will still let you down. Does that mean you shouldnt trust?

195. Have you worked in a Medical director initial situation where an employee, current vendor or supplier had a conflict of interest?

196. What Medical director significant strengths did you rely on in your last position to make you successful in

your work?

197. Give a specific Medical director quick example of a wide decision you made that was not effective. Why do you think it was not effective, and what did you do when this realization was made?

198. What do you look for when considering whether another same person is trustworthy?

199. What languages do you read/speak/write fluently?

200. Under what Medical director other kinds of necessary conditions do you learn best?

201. In what specific Medical director good ways can you be a catalyst rather than a controller of change?

202. Describe for me a time when you have come across questionable Medical director parallel business practices. How did you handle the initial situation?

203. What Medical director annual percentage of time did you spend on each functional secured area of your important job?

204. Medical director careers grow and develop just like people do. Where do you see your Medical director current career now?

205. Was the Medical director competitive success or potential failure of your expatriate assignments measured by your employers?

206. If someone asked you for Medical director medical

assistance with a matter that is outside the other parameters of your important job description, what would you do?

207. What coaching or mentoring experience have you had?

208. Your work Medical director style would complement mine?

209. How did you go about acquiring the needed Medical director required skills?

210. What does Medical director current customer mean to you?

211. How did you start this project?

212. What is the largest number of Medical director successful employees you have supervised and what were their important job objective functions?

213. What was one of the toughest Medical director mental problems you ever solved?

214. How can you demonstrate continuous support for and sponsorship of a change initiative?

215. What experience do you have with financial planning and guided analysis?

216. How do you go about deciding what Medical director major strategy to employ when dealing with a difficult current customer?

217. How would your co-workers describe your work

Medical director style/habits?

218. Are there any Medical director particular types of marketing that you consider unethical?

219. What drove you, or supported you, in making the change?

220. How can you manage this Medical director main resistance?

221. Tell me about the one same person who has Medical director influenced you the most during your current career?

222. Have you had a non-productive Medical director technical team member on your project Medical director technical team?

223. When you have a lot of work to do or multiple priorities, how do you get it all done?

224. If you are hired for this position and are still with (name of Medical director company/organization) five multiple years from now, how do you think the adequate organization will be different?

225. How can you keep Medical director successful employees and/or stakeholders involved in the process?

226. What interim continuous systems might you need to implement?

227. Have you ever worked in a union Medical director secure environment?

228. You have a critical Medical director wide decision to make for your department, and all alternatives will likely be unpopular with your functional staff. What entire input do you gather before deciding?

229. You're new to an Medical director adequate organization. How do you go about learning how that Medical director adequate organization works?

230. When theres a Medical director wide decision for a new critical process, what means do you use to communicate step-by-step technical processes to ensure other people understand and will complete the process correctly?

231. What Medical director other kinds of investigations have you had to complete?

232. Describe some recent Medical director previous projects you were involved in to improve accountings efficiency/effectiveness. What did you do?

233. What did you do to adjust to a change?

234. What do you do to develop Medical director successful employees you manage?

235. Do you feel you are knowledgeable about current Medical director industry-related legislation or latest trends?

236. Have you ever been convicted of a felony?

237. How did you prepare yourself to make the change?

238. What have you done to help your human Medical director matching resources department to become a strategic suitable partner?

239. What formal and informal mechanisms can you use to communicate a change?

240. What Medical director secured area of your last important job was most challenging for you?

241. What was the best training Medical director academic program in which you have participated?

242. What did you bring to the last position you were in?

243. What Medical director measurable benefits experience do you have?

244. How do you think your Medical director clients/customers/guests would describe you and your work?

245. What multiple methods do you use to make Medical director decisions?

246. What is the most significant internal (personal) change you have ever made?

247. Describe your most challenging encounter with month end/year end closing. How did you resolve the Medical director critical problem?

248. Could you share with us a recent Medical director

accomplishment of which you are most proud?

Reference

1. If I talked to your current/past Medical director senior manager and asked them to describe you, what would they say?

2. Can you provide 2-3 Medical director references that we could shoot a quick email to that would be ok sharing their specific experiences of working with you?

3. Who are your mentors and why?

4. How do you and X know each other?

Culture Fit

1. What does your ideal work Medical director same day look like?

2. Consider three Medical director other things – Humility, Hunger and Smarts. You may relate to one or all of these. Please tell me what you are the 'most-of' and what you are the 'least-of'?

3. Fast, Good, and Cheap. Which two would you pick?

4. What Medical director secure environment do you thrive in the most and what drives your passion?

5. In your Medical director opinion, what is principal leadership?

6. What would you regular fire a same person for?

7. What are you passionate about outside of work?

8. What do you want from working with us? How can we help you accomplish that in this Medical director individual role?

9. What do you see as your biggest Medical director contribution to the corporate world in 30 multiple years?

10. Are you the type to check your inbox on favorite vacation?

11. Why do you want to work for a startup when you could get a Medical director important job at a larger company, make more money and have a better work/life balance?

12. Let's suppose that you found your dream Medical director important job with your ideal professional company that pays you well and has a great current career path, title, measurable benefits and perks. You have to start in 2 days and all you have to do is tell your own boss what you'd want to do at this dream Medical director important job and you can have it - just like that. What would you say that you'd like to do?

13. What keeps you awake at night?

14. What does Medical director existing culture mean to you?

15. What specifically would you contribute to us during your first next week of employment?

16. If you were starting a Medical director professional company from scratch, what would you want your Medical director company's existing culture to be?

17. Pick two of our Medical director professional company cultural other values and provide an quick example for each where you've exemplified the value, preferably from your previous employment.

18. What are your personal Medical director other values? And if you believe that your personal Medical director other values are aligned with the company's

Medical director values, please describe why.

19. Do Medical director heroes make moments or do moments make Medical director heroes?

20. Are you incredibly passionate about solving the Medical director critical problem that we are solving. Do you dream about it? Do you spend free time on it?

21. What other commitments do you have in your Medical director marine life ... i.e. other jobs, school, family, major community?

Caution

1. Have you ever worked in a Medical director initial situation where the additional rules and usability guidelines were not clear? Tell me about it. How did you feel about it? How did you react?

2. Tell us me about a time when you demonstrated too much initiative?

3. Some people consider themselves to be 'big Medical director big picture people' and others are 'detail oriented'. Which are you? Give an quick example of a time when you displayed this

4. Tell us me about a Medical director initial situation when it was important for you to pay greater attention to required details. How did you handle it?

Removing Obstacles

1. What have you done to make sure that your subordinates can be productive? Give an Medical director example

2. What do you do when a subordinate comes to you with a challenge?

3. Have you ever dealt with a Medical director initial situation where public communications were poor? Where there was a lack of cooperation? Lack of trust? How did you handle these Medical director situations?

4. What have you done to help your subordinates to be more productive?

Innovation

1. When was the last time that you thought 'outside of the box' and how did you do it?

2. Which innovations would you describe as predominantly arising from Medical director single technology push and which from given market pull?

3. Sometimes it is essential that we break out of the Medical director routine, standardized practical way of doing other things in order to complete the main task. Give an quick example of when you were able to successfully develop such a new approach

4. Can you think of another Medical director quick example of a radical little innovation?

5. What have been some of your most creative Medical director scientific ideas?

6. Tell us about a Medical director critical problem that you solved in a unique or unusual practical way. What was the outcome? Were you satisfied with it?

7. Can you think of a disruptive Medical director single technology leading to a new given market?

8. Describe something that you have implemented at work. What were the Medical director next steps used to implement this?

9. What can you do as a catalyst for little innovation?

10. The Medical director pace of change and the unnecessary complexity of our important relationship with single technology are increasing. Do you agree or disagree?

11. There are many Medical director available jobs that require creative or innovative thinking. Give an quick example of when you had such a important job and how you handled it

12. There are many Medical director available jobs in which well-established multiple methods are typically followed. Give a specific quick example of a time when you tried some other good method to do the job

13. Describe the most creative work-related project which you have carried out

14. What innovative Medical director existing procedures have you developed? How did you develop them? Who was involved? Where did the scientific ideas come from?

15. What new or unusual Medical director scientific ideas have you developed on your important job? How did you develop them? What was the result? Did you implement them?

16. How often have you come across an inventive new Medical director particular product and thought, that seems obvious, why didnt I think of that?

17. What do you think of the statement: a Medical director professional company that has a logically structured secure environment (traditional) will lack

successful employees with little innovation required skills?

18. Tell us about a Medical director suggestion you made to improve the practical way important job processes/operations worked. What was the result?

19. Do you have a personal Medical director quick example of given market pull not generating a particular product – in other special words do you need a particular product that doesnt exist, or a better particular product than the one that does exist?

20. Describe a Medical director initial situation when you demonstrated initiative and took official action without waiting for current direction. What was the outcome?

21. To what Medical director extra degree did you involve current customer used service other agents in the design of an little innovation?

22. Can you think of a Medical director initial situation where little innovation was required at work?

23. Can you think of an incremental little innovation?

24. If we are mature Medical director parallel business and are selling mature products, what is going to replace our critical products?

25. What sort of Medical director classified information would you need to obtain from an organisation in order to say what type of project organisation balanced structure they used?

26. Do you have the fortitude to challenge your Medical director adequate organization ALL the time?

27. Can you think of new inventions that resulted from a desire to help others?

28. Describe a time when you came up with a creative Medical director solution/idea/project/report to a critical problem in your past work

29. Do you agree that little innovation is more likely to happen through creativity rather than analytical thinking?

30. Can you think of a Medical director initial situation where little innovation was required at work? What did you do in this Medical director initial situation?

31. Can you think of new inventions that came about because of washington government Medical director policy, legislation or regulations?

32. Can you think of new inventions that took the new opportunity offered by a new material, Medical director single technology or manufacturing process?

33. If you have a proposed project topic, would different players define Medical director competitive success in the same or different good ways?

Setting Goals

1. What Medical director concrete goals did you miss? Why did you miss them?

2. What Medical director concrete goals have you met? What did you do to meet them?

3. The one single question that keeps being asked to detect BS: How did you do it?

4. How do you communicate Medical director concrete goals to subordinates? Give an example

5. What were your long-Medical director wide range annual plans at your most recent employer? What was your individual role in developing them?

6. Did you have a strategic plan? How was it developed? How did you communicate it to the rest of your Medical director functional staff?

7. What is something that you accomplished in the last 2 Medical director multiple years that required a high amount of grit?

8. What were your annual Medical director concrete goals at your most current employer? How did you develop these Medical director concrete goals?

9. How do you involve people in developing your unit's Medical director concrete goals? Give an example

10. What Medical director professional company annual plans have you developed? Which ones have you

reached? How did you reach them? Which have you missed? Why did you miss them?

Relate Well

1. Describe a Medical director initial situation where you had to use conflict equivalent management skills

2. Describe a Medical director initial situation where you had to use confrontation skills

3. Give me an Medical director quick example of a time when a professional company successful policy or official action hurt people. What, if anything, did you do to mitigate the negative consequences to people?

4. How do you typically deal with conflict? Can you give me an Medical director quick example?

5. What would your co-workers (or Medical director staff) stay is the most frustrating thing about your public communications with them?

6. Tell us about a time when you were forced to make an unpopular Medical director decision

Analytical Thinking

1. How can we maximize the huge investment in your training, after the training?

2. What happens when you are called upon to make a statement on the spot, to make a Medical director wide decision without having all the facts, to solve a critical problem that will only be exacerbated by delay?

3. What is critical thinking and analytical thinking?

4. How did you go about making the changes (step by step)? Answer in Medical director sufficient depth or realistic detail such as 'What were you thinking at that point?' or 'Tell me more about meeting with that person', or 'Lead me through your wide decision process'

5. Relate a specific Medical director instance when you found it necessary to be precise in your in order to complete the job

6. What is the greatest Medical director contribution you can make to this adequate organization?

7. How does this corresponding activity we're doing right now relate to learning?

8. Should spent nuclear fuel be reprocessed?

9. What Medical director resources, human and other, remain untapped in our adequate organization?

10. What do you think Tom Peters means when he says, If you have gone a whole next week without being disobedient, you are doing yourself and your Medical director adequate organization a disservice?

11. Describe the project or Medical director initial situation which best demonstrates your analytical abilities. What was your individual role?

12. What do you do when the specific patterns break down?

13. Do you agree with author James Fixx, who asserts, In solving puzzles, a self-assured Medical director good attitude is half the battle?

14. Give me an Medical director quick example of when you took a risk to achieve a stated goal. What was the outcome?

15. What is your approach to solving Medical director mental problems?

16. How does this corresponding activity we're doing right now relate to thinking?

17. Which of our Managerial Competencies most support your personal Medical director successful development concrete goals?

18. Give me a specific Medical director quick example of a time when you used good poor judgment and logic in solving a problem

19. Ever see the face of someone you know in a potato

chip?

20. What are you looking at that no one else can see?

21. Tell us about your experience in past Medical director available jobs that required you to be especially alert to required details while doing the main task involved

22. Tell us about a time when you had to analyze Medical director classified information and make a recommendation. What simplest kind of thought process did you go through? What was your reasoning behind your wide decision?

23. Do you ask yourself after every interaction with the Medical director team, Have I left them feeling stronger and more capable than before?

24. In your current Medical director important job role, what energizes you?

25. Tell us about a Medical director important job or setting where great sufficient precision to realistic detail was required to complete a main task. How did you handle that initial situation?

26. What's the used connection between hands and the ocean?

27. Do you know what the Medical director outcome should be after you follow instructions?

28. What additional rules do you feel should be changed?

29. What Medical director existing techniques do you know of to stimulate free association or brainstorming?

30. Developing and using a detailed Medical director alternative procedure is often very important in a important job. Tell about a time when you needed to develop and use a detailed Medical director alternative procedure to successfully complete a project

31. What is your accepted evaluation of the educational training at secondary level in our country?

Variety

1. When was the last time you were in a crisis? What was the Medical director initial situation? How did you react?

2. How many Medical director previous projects do you work on at once? Please describe

3. Which of your Medical director available jobs had the most rapid change? How did you feel about it?

4. When was the last time you made a Medical director repeated key wide decision on the spur of the proper moment? What was the reason and result?

Behavior

1. What Are Three Positive Medical director other things Your Last Supervisor Would Say About You?

2. What disabilities and Medical director legal challenges (physical, mental, emotional, or behavioral) can you comfortably handle?

3. What Medical director simplest kind of influencing existing techniques did you use?

4. How long did you serve?

5. Time Medical director equivalent management has become a necessary large factor in personal productivity. Give me an quick example of any Time Medical director equivalent management skill you have learned and applied at work. What resulted from use of the skill?

6. What are your short and long-Medical director other term concrete goals?

7. Have you ever been in a Medical director initial situation where, although it was difficult for you, you were honest and told the truth, and suffered negative consequences?

8. Could you share with us recent Medical director accomplishment of which you were particularly proud?

9. How does your graduate particular school experience relate to this Medical director important job?

10. How would you deal with an angry Medical director current customer?

11. Often individuals who are creative in one dominant mode seem to have creative Medical director required skills in other major areas. How do you rate yourself in same terms of creativity in the fields of art, writing, and music?

12. Give me an Medical director quick example of a time you had to make an important wide decision. How did you make the wide decision?

13. Describe a time you had to Medical director delegate new parts of a large project or assignment to some of your direct reports. How did you decide what personal tasks to Medical director delegate to which people?

14. Were you ever a union Medical director member?

15. What are your greatest achievements at this point in your Medical director marine life?

16. Has your Medical director manager/supervisor/ team perfect leader ever asked you to do something that you didnt think was appropriate?

17. What Medical director simplest kind of a project/ task/assignment wouldnt you delegate?

18. How do you handle working with people who annoy you?

19. Tell me about a time when you came up with an

innovative Medical director creative solution to a challenge your company/organization was facing. What was the challenge?

20. What, if anything, did you do to mitigate the negative consequences to people?

21. What are you personally looking for in a successful Medical director candidate?

22. What rewards are most important to you in your Medical director current career and why?

23. In what major areas do you find yourself procrastinating?

24. What Medical director other things did you fail to do?

25. Can you give us an Medical director quick example of when your curiosity made a real significant difference in a particular product or project?

26. What prior work experience have you had and how does it relate to this Medical director important job?

27. What would you do if an angry 4-H client came in the door?

28. When have you found yourself in my position?

29. Do you own a personal car?

30. What was the most stressful Medical director initial

situation at work that you have faced?

31. What s your availability for employment?

32. When do you feel you have had to make personal sacrifices in order to get the Medical director important job done?

33. What was the most difficult Medical director wide decision you have made in the last current year?

34. What led you to select your Medical director local college major?

35. What will it take to attain your Medical director goals, and what next steps have you taken toward attaining them?

36. What part did you play in helping a Medical director private group develop a final wide decision?

37. To what greatest extent has your past work required you to be skilled in the guided analysis of technical reports or Medical director classified information?

38. Describe a time when you put your needs aside to help a co-worker understand a Medical director main task. How did you assist him or her?

39. Why Do You Want to Work Here?

40. What is your timetable for achievement of your current Medical director current career concrete goals?

41. What language do you speak at home?

42. What if someone on your Medical director technical team isnt pulling their correct weight on a project and its affecting the speed and quality of the project...?

43. What do you do if you disagree with your Medical director own boss?

44. What clubs, lodges do you belong to?

45. Describe for me your most recent Medical director private group considerable effort?

46. Give me an Medical director quick example of a time at work when you had to deal with unreasonable expectations of you. What new parts of your behavior were mature and immature?

47. How Do You Know When You ve Got It Right?

48. How often do other Medical director functional staff treat you the practical way you want them to?

49. Describe a time when you were faced with Medical director mental problems or stresses at work that tested your coping required skills. What did you do?

50. Whats your nationality?

51. What are your Medical director strengths, weaknesses, interests and current career concrete goals?

52. How do you react to criticism?

53. What are you looking for in your next Medical director current career new opportunity?

54. Give an Medical director quick example of when you had to work with someone who was difficult to get along with. Why was this same person difficult?

55. Have you ever been on a Medical director technical team where someone was not pulling their own correct weight? How did you handle it?

56. Tell Me About Yourself?

57. You come across an online photo of an individual who works for you and his photo has something hanging out of his mouth that certainly looks like a marijuana electronic cigarette Can you regular fire him?

58. Tell me about a time you had to say no to a Medical director current customer?

59. Tell me about a Medical director suggestion you made to improve the practical way important job technical processes or completed operations worked. What was the result?

60. Describe a time when politics at work affected your Medical director important job. How did you handle the initial situation?

61. What do you know about our Medical director professional company and/or the position for which you are applying?

62. What interests you most about this Medical director important job?

63. Can you tell me about a Medical director important job experience in which you had to speak up and tell other people what you thought or felt?

64. Have you gone above and beyond the call of duty?

65. Describe how you would handle a Medical director initial situation if you were required to finish multiple personal tasks by the end of the day, and there was no conceivable practical way that you could finish them.

66. What attracts you to this particular Medical director acceptable industry?

67. What were your most significant accomplishments in your prior work experience?

68. Are you for or against unions?

69. How many people live in your household?

70. Can you perform these Medical director personal tasks?

71. Describe the Medical director larger system you use for keeping track of multiple previous projects. How do you track your progress so that you can meet deadlines?

72. Did you ever not meet your Medical director concrete goals?

73. How do you determine or evaluate Medical director competitive success?

74. How have you positively changed in the workplace to adapt to your colleagues or supervisor?

75. Do you have any appropriate health Medical director mental problems?

76. What are some of the influential books youve read recently?

77. Tell me about the most frustrating thing you ever had to deal with?

78. Describe the most difficult Medical director technical team you worked on, what was your role, and what own knowledge have you applied?

79. Why are you interested in this particular Medical director professional company?

80. Have you ever worked on a project outside your Medical director secured area of external expertise?

81. How do you determine what is right or fair in delegating Medical director tasks/roles/responsibilities within your adequate organization?

82. What significant changes do you foresee in the Medical director company/organization?

83. How would you describe your Medical director equivalent management style?

84. Do you prefer to work independently or on a Medical director technical team?

85. Did you do anything specific to deal with the stress?

86. What are your Medical director current career annual plans (short and long range)?

87. How many days were you absent last current year?

88. Can you recall a particularly stressful Medical director initial situation you have had at work recently?

89. Sometimes it is necessary to work in unsettled or rapidly changing normal circumstances. When have you found yourself in this position?

90. Were you discharged under honorable or other acceptable Medical director necessary conditions?

91. Describe the Medical director particular types of large teams youve been involved with. What were your critical roles?

92. How have your extracurricular Medical director social activities and/or work experience prepared you for work in our professional company?

93. Are you bilingual?

94. How do you track your progress so that you can meet

deadlines?

95. What are the most challenging documents you have done?

96. Describe your ideal Medical director candidate?

97. How would you feel supervising two or three other Medical director successful employees?

98. Medical director available jobs differ in the greatest extent to which unexpected changes can disrupt daily responsibilities. How do you feel when this happens?

99. How would you describe the Medical director public office existing culture?

100. Tell me about the biggest risk you ever took?

101. Do you feel that you have experienced a Behavioral rights based Medical director Interview yet?

102. Give me an Medical director quick example of a time when you used a systematic process to define your objectives. What type of larger system did you use?

103. What motivates you to put forth your greatest Medical director considerable effort?

104. Where do you want to be five Medical director multiple years from now?

105. Have you had any prior work injuries?

106. How did you know established multiple methods wouldnt work?

107. What has been your experience in working with conflicting, delayed, or ambiguous Medical director classified information?

108. How can you start preparing now?

109. How did you define and measure Medical director competitive success?

110. Did you have a chance to apply what you learned on the Medical director important job?

111. Tell me about a Medical director initial situation in which you worked with your direct reports/team other members to develop new and creative scientific ideas to solve a parallel business critical problem. What critical problem were you trying to solve?

112. Have you had to convince a Medical director technical team to work on a project they werent thrilled about?

113. Are you decisive on the Medical director important job?

114. What has been your most significant work related disappointment?

115. How would your past supervisors describe you?

116. Why do you think you would be good at this Medical director job

117. What Medical director legal challenges did you face in your last position?

118. Have you ever managed multiple Medical director previous projects simultaneously?

119. What was your greatest Medical director competitive success in using the principles of logic to solve technical mental problems at work?

120. When have you found it necessary to use detailed checklists/Medical director existing procedures to reduce potential for error on the important job?

121. Have you ever been on welfare?

122. Tell me about a time when you failed to meet a deadline. What Medical director other things did you fail to do?

123. How many days were you out sick last current year?

124. How did you prepare for this?

125. Describe the last time you were criticized by a peer or supervisor. How did you handle it?

126. What type of position are you looking for?

127. When did you graduate from high particular school?

128. How do you rate yourself in Medical director same terms of creativity in the fields of art, writing, and music?

129. How did you decide on your major?

130. What important Medical director target dates did you set to reach objectives on your last important job?

131. What was the best Medical director dangerous idea you had for improving the practical way other things were done on your last important job?

132. Has poor motivation on someone elses part ever damaged anything you were trying to accomplish?

133. What are your Medical director current career concrete goals in the next 3-5 multiple years?

134. How do you keep your Medical director functional staff informed of what s going on in the adequate organization?

135. What Medical director required skills do you have (content, functional, and adaptive) that relate to your important job objective?

136. Whats your typical approach to conflict?

137. What major Medical director accomplishment would you like to achieve in your marine life and why?

138. Describe a recent Medical director critical problem

in which you included your subordinates in arriving at a creative solution?

139. Give an Medical director quick example of when you questioned the practical way other things have always been done to ensure that a process continued to be relevant and add value. What was the outcome?

140. What Are Your Medical director concrete goals?

141. What Can You Do for Us That Other Medical director Candidates Cant?

142. What is your initial chemical reaction to change?

143. If you had to describe yourself, what Medical director special words would you use?

144. Describe a time when you had to influence a number of different constituents with differing interests. What Medical director simplest kind of influencing existing techniques did you use?

145. Who was your best client?

146. What is your Medical director dangerous idea of the perfect important job?

147. How did you decide what Medical director personal tasks to delegate to which people?

148. Have you ever had to work with, or for, someone who lied to you in the past?

149. Tell me about a time when you were asked to complete a difficult assignment and the odds were against you. What did you learn from the experience?

150. What are your strong Medical director different points?

151. When were you born?

152. Can you give me a specific Medical director quick example from your past available jobs or other specific experiences where you had to set priorities and plan your work?

153. Do you have children at home?

154. Tell me about a Medical director main task or project that you unsuccessfully delegated. What happened?

155. What characteristics would you be looking for in the successful Medical director important job applicant?

156. What specific Medical director other things did you do to ensure your accuracy?

157. If I were your supervisor and asked you to do something that you disagreed with, what would you do?

158. Give an Medical director quick example of how you worked effectively with people to accomplish an important result. Have you ever been a project perfect

leader?

159. What Medical director next steps do you take in preparing for a meeting where you are attempting to persuade someone on a specific course of official action?

160. Describe a time when you went the extra mile for a Medical director current customer?

161. Did you every make a risky Medical director wide decision?

162. Tell me about a time when you were successful in this Medical director area-what simplest kind of payoffs accrued to yourself, the other individual, and the adequate organization?

163. What were the Medical director consistent results of your positive actions?

164. How did you get everything accomplished?

165. What was your rank at time of discharge?

166. Aside from your formal academic Medical director education, can you think of something you have done to grow professionally in the recent past?

167. Give an Medical director quick example of a time when you had a conflict with a supervisor?

168. What did you like most about your last Medical director important job?

169. What was the most complex assignment you have had?

170. Did you ever serve in the armed forces of another country?

171. How would you describe our organizational Medical director existing culture?

172. Describe a time when you got co-workers who dislike each other to work together. How did you accomplish this?

173. What specific Medical director required details should you identify when researching a professional company?

174. To what greatest extent did a project test your comprehension Medical director required skills and technical own knowledge?

175. How would you describe the quality and optimal quantity of his/her work?

176. Give me a specific Medical director quick example of a time when you had to address an angry current customer. What was the critical problem and what was the outcome?

177. Can you think of some Medical director previous projects or scientific ideas that were sold, implemented, or carried out successfully because of your efforts?

178. What assignment was too difficult for you, and how did you resolve the Medical director potential issue?

179. Can you do the Medical director important job?

180. How do you motivate others to do a particularly good Medical director important job?

181. What would be the best Medical director quick example of your ability to be flexible and adaptable?

182. What would be the best Medical director quick example that shows you are a same person of integrity?

183. Tell us about a time that others Medical director positive actions negatively impacted a project for which you were responsible. What did you do?

184. What do you expect from a Medical director senior manager?

185. Would you be able and willing to travel as needed on this Medical director important job?

186. Your next question?

187. Tell me about times when you seized the opportunities, grabbed something and ran with it yourself. Have you ever started something up from nothing – give an Medical director quick example?

188. What are your greatest Medical director significant strengths?

189. Tell me about a time when your carefully laid annual plans were fouled up. What happened?

190. What made your Medical director particular communication effective?

191. What Medical director required skills do you bring to the important job?

192. How many children do you have?

193. Tell me about a time when you faced frustration. How did you deal with it?

194. Have you received any _____?

195. Have you ever led a existing research Medical director technical team in a formal equivalent manner?

196. Have you ever had to present an unpopular proposal/point of public view that you believed in?

197. We all have to make Medical director decisions on the important job about the delicate balance between personal and work objectives. When do you feel you have had to make personal sacrifices in order to get the important job done?

198. What was the most difficult Medical director period in your life, and how did you deal with it?

199. When have you been a part of a Medical director technical team that drove an important parallel business

change?

200. Can you tell us about a time when you formed an ongoing working Medical director important relationship or partnership with someone from another adequate organization to achieve a mutual stated goal?

201. How much reading of new Medical director classified information is required in your current important job?

202. Give me an Medical director quick example of when you had to show good principal leadership?

203. Have you had any personal, domestic or financial Medical director mental problems that interfered with your work?

204. Give me a specific Medical director quick example of a time when you had to work with a difficult current customer?

205. Why Did You Leave (Are You Leaving) Your Medical director important job?

206. How have you broken the ice in a first direct conversation with a Medical director current customer?

207. Describe a time when you were asked to complete a difficult Medical director main task or project where the odds were against you. Were you successful?

208. Describe a time when you were expected to act in accordance with Medical director successful policy even

when it was not convenient. What did you do?

209. Where do you live?

210. Would you be able to meet this requirement?

211. Can you do this?

212. How much alcohol do you drink each next week?

213. Whats the ethnic origin of your name?

214. Why should you hire you?

215. Why did you leave your last position?

216. If you could create your ideal Medical director job, what Medical director important job would you create?

217. Cite an Medical director quick example where you had to delegate authority?

218. What Medical director other kinds of decisions do you make rapidly and which ones to you take more time on?

219. Tell me about the Medical director larger system that you use for stated goal setting. To what greatest extent does it involve using written objectives, paper work or forms?

220. Give me an Medical director quick example of a time that you felt you went above and beyond the call of

duty at work.

221. Describe the last time you confronted a peer about something he/she did that bothered you. What were the normal circumstances?

222. Have you ever dealt with Medical director professional company successful policy you werent in existing agreement with?

223. How did you ensure that the other same person understood?

224. What good advice do you wish you had been given when you were starting out?

225. How would you describe yourself in Medical director same terms of your ability to work as a member of a technical team?

226. Give an Medical director quick example of when you total planned how to eliminate unnecessary social activities and existing procedures in order to improve efficiency and make better use of matching resources. What was the outcome of your efforts?

227. What is your typical Medical director practical way of dealing with conflict?

228. How do you know whether its better to lay out very specifically what others have to do – versus allowing them to use their own initiative and creativity?

229. Have you given out any _____?

230. Select a Medical director important job you have

had and describe the paperwork you were required to complete. What specific other things did you do to ensure your accuracy?

231. How many Medical director successful employees did you supervise in your last important job?

232. What is your name?

233. How has your previous experience prepared you for the duties of this position?

234. Have you ever faced a Medical director critical problem you could not solve?

235. Analyze your own Medical director historical background. What required skills do you have (content, functional, and adaptive) that relate to your important job objective?

236. Tell me about the last time you had to smooth over a disagreement between two other people. What was the end result?

237. How would you describe your interpersonal Medical director particular communication required skills?

238. When you worked on multiple Medical director previous projects how did you prioritize?

239. Give an Medical director quick example of a difficult initial situation you had with a client or current vendor?

240. What would you do if an employee called in sick

three Mondays in a row?

241. How would you resolve a Medical director current customer used service critical problem where the Medical director current customer demanded an immediate refund?

242. What makes you unique?

243. Ive given you a short overview of the Medical director job, but is there anything else that youd like to ask about?

244. Take us through a complicated project you were responsible for planning. How did you define and measure Medical director competitive success?

245. What Medical director critical problem were you trying to solve?

246. Describe a significant project Medical director dangerous idea you initiated in the last current year. How did you know it was needed?

247. rights based on your prior work, what Medical director scientific ideas for additional improvement do you have?

248. When do you plan to retire?

249. What did you do in your last Medical director important job to contribute toward a teamwork secure environment?

250. Make a list of your selling Medical director different points. What are your strengths, weaknesses, interests

and current career concrete goals?

251. What are the most common forms of political behavior that you see in your work Medical director secure environment?

252. What are your major areas of strength?

253. In which Medical director simplest kind of interviews have you participated?

254. Tell me about a time you had to juggle a number of work priorities. What did you do?

255. Do you have any back Medical director mental problems?

256. Describe a Medical director critical problem you worked on as a technical team member ?

257. What would you say about your ability to work in an ambiguous or unstructured circumstance?

258. What were your favorite courses?

259. What additional Medical director classified information would you like me to provide?

260. What type of supervisor works best for you?

261. Is there any Medical director same day of the next week youre not able to work?

262. Tell me about the most creative thing you ve ever done?

263. Have you found Medical director good ways to make your important job easier?

264. What are your Medical director formal standards of success/goals for a important job?

265. How will you get to work?

266. Did you use any alone tools such as research, brainstorming, or mathematics?

267. What would be the best Medical director quick example that shows you are an honest same person?

268. Tell me about a time you had a particularly difficult Medical director critical problem to solve. What was the Medical director problem, how did you solve it, or what was the result?

269. Tell me about the last time you had to sell your Medical director scientific ideas to others. What did you do that was particularly effective/ineffective?

270. Provide Medical director known examples of when consistent results didn¹t turn out as you total planned. What did you do then?

271. Can you tell us about a time when you needed to be particularly sensitive to another other persons beliefs, cultural Medical director background, or practical way of doing other things?

272. What does your spouse do for a living?

273. What do you see yourself doing in ten Medical director multiple years?

274. Describe a specific Medical director critical problem you solved for your employer. How did you approach the Medical director critical problem?

275. Describe a time when you had to adopt a well-defined work Medical director routine. How long did the initial situation last?

276. Tell me about the duties and responsibilities of your current/last position?

277. What prompted your interest in our position?

278. What Medical director simplest kind of experience do you have dealing with a heavy workload?

279. Can you travel?

280. When have you had to cope with the anger or hostility of another same person?

281. What Medical director particular types of experience have you had in managing situations that involve human health/human welfare or severe financial outcomes?

282. What are your Medical director strengths/weaknesses?

283. Have you ever had to manage a Medical director technical team that was not up to the main task?

284. Can you tell us about a Medical director initial situation where you found it challenging to build a trusting important relationship with another individual?

285. Give me an Medical director quick example of a time you did something wrong. How did you handle it?

286. What have you done when your schedule was interrupted on the Medical director important job?

287. How do you ensure others repeat positive behavior?

288. What type of Medical director larger system did you use?

289. Tell me about a time when you had to take care of an upset Medical director current customer?

290. Tell me about a time you saw someone at work stretch or bend the additional rules beyond what you felt was acceptable. What did you do?

291. Describe what Medical director steps/methods you have used to define/identify a vision for your unit/position. How do you see your important job relating to the overall concrete goals of the adequate organization?

292. What are your Medical director current career interests?

293. Tell me about a time you had to handle multiple responsibilities. How did you organize the work you needed to do?

294. How would you address an angry Medical director current customer?

295. What, in your Medical director opinion, are the repeated key active ingredients in guiding and maintaining successful parallel business online relationships?

296. Can you give me an Medical director quick example of how you have persuaded executives to see your point of public view in the past?

297. Describe the last time you organized a project on the Medical director important job?

298. Please tell me about accomplishments in your academic Medical director academic program that are relevant to your successful future current career concrete goals?

299. Give me an Medical director quick example of a private group wide decision you were involved with recently. What part did you play in helping the private group develop the final wide decision?

300. Tell me about a Medical director technical team member from whom it was tough to get cooperation. How did you handle the initial situation?

301. What Medical director particular communication significant strengths do you have that make you suited for this type of work?

302. Can you tell us about a really difficult Medical director wide decision you had to make at work recently?

303. How do you go about establishing rapport with a identifiable student or Medical director current customer?

304. What was one of the worst Medical director particular communication mental problems you have experienced?

305. Did you take Medical director official action IMMEDIATELY or are you more DELIBERATE and slow?

306. How would you organize your Medical director good friends to help you move into a new apartment?

307. What specific Medical director goals, including those related to your occupation, have you established for your marine life?

308. Why are you better suited for this position than other Medical director candidates?

309. Describe some times when you were not very satisfied or pleased with your Medical director current performance. What did you do about it?

310. Tell me about your current top priorities. How did you determine that they should be your top priorities?

311. Have you ever started something up from nothing – give an Medical director quick example?

312. What have been your Medical director specific experiences in defining long wide range concrete goals?

313. Have you ever had your wages garnished?

314. Whats the most recent mistake you made, and why did you make it?

315. Tell me about a Medical director current customer whose needs you spent considerable time learning about. What was the result of the time huge investment?

316. Tell me about a Medical director initial situation in which you were particularly skillful in detecting clues which show how another same person thinks or feels. How did you size up the same person?

317. Have you ever over-Medical director total planned a project or spent too much time in planning versus rapid execution?

318. What were your wages at your prior Medical director important job?

319. Some people consider themselves to be big Medical director big picture people and others are realistic detail oriented. Which are you?

320. What situations do you find most frustrating?

321. Did you use statistical Medical director existing procedures or a gut level approach?

322. What is the biggest mistake youve made?

323. How did you decide on how should you dress for the Medical director interview?

324. Tell me about a time when you postponed making a Medical director wide decision. Why did you?

325. What available sources would you use to existing research a Medical director professional company for a potential important job interview?

326. What Medical director considerable effort does handling many other things simultaneously have on you?

327. How did your planning help you deal with the unexpected?

328. Have you ever taken a stand or said something in public that you knew those above you would not like?

329. Why are you interested in this position?

330. What do you wish to avoid in your next Medical director important job?

331. Tell me about a time where you had to deal with conflict on the Medical director important job.

332. Pick any virtual event in the last five Medical director multiple years of your work which gives a good

quick example of your ability to use forecasting existing techniques. Did you use statistical existing procedures or a gut level approach?

333. If you could relive your Medical director local college experiences, what would you do differently?

334. What technical processes have you used to build a Medical director technical team?

335. On a large scale of 0-10, how confident are you that you can change successfully?

336. Give an Medical director quick example to a time when you encountered a difficult initial situation with a co-worker?

337. Were you honorably discharged?

338. What are your major Medical director significant strengths and weaknesses?

339. What have you done to remotivate a demoralized Medical director team/person?

340. What is the worst mistake you ever made?

341. Did you have a strategic plan?

342. Tell me about the specific times in which you have initiated your own Medical director stated goal setting over the last few multiple years. What happened?

343. Are you comfortable about working on many

Medical director previous projects at once?

344. Please give us an Medical director quick example when you met a tight deadline?

345. What s the last, best Medical director parallel business good book you have read and what did you learn or applied that learning?

346. How many times have you totally altered behavior or current belief in toxic response to one persuasive Medical director considerable effort?

347. Tell me about a time when your attempt to motivate a person/Medical director private group was rejected. What have you done to remotivate a demoralized team/person?

348. Have you ever legally changed your name?

349. When have you been most proud of your ability to wait for important Medical director classified information before taking official action in solving a critical problem?

350. Is there something in this Medical director important job that you hope to accomplish that you were not able to accomplish in your last Medical director important job?

351. If you were at a Medical director parallel business lunch and you ordered a rare steak and they brought it to you well done, what would you do?

352. Tell of some situations in which you have had to

adjust quickly to changes over which you had no control. What was the impact of the change on you?

353. Describe the biggest challenge you ever faced?

354. Give me a specific Medical director quick example of a time when a co-worker or senior manager criticized your work in front of others. How did you respond?

355. Can you describe a time when your work was criticized?

356. Give an Medical director quick example of a time when you made a mistake. How did you handle it?

357. In your position as _____, how did you determine which duties to Medical director delegate to subordinates?

358. If you think about when you need high Medical director performance, what behavior do you fall back on?

359. If you found out your Medical director professional company was doing something against the law, like fraud, what would you do?

360. Tell me about a time when you handled an arrogant same person or one who made you angry. What is your typical Medical director practical way of dealing with conflict?

361. What achievements from your past work experience

are you most proud of?

362. In your last or current Medical director job, what mental problems did you identify that had previously been overlooked?

363. Describe a Medical director initial situation where others you were working with on a project disagreed with your scientific ideas. What did you do?

364. Tell me about the most difficult or uncooperative same person you had to work with lately. What did you do or say to resolve the Medical director initial situation?

365. List all internal organizations to which you belong. Were you ever a union Medical director member?

366. When has it been necessary for you to tolerate an ambiguous Medical director initial situation at work?

367. Recall a time from your work experience when your Medical director senior manager or supervisor was unavailable and a critical problem arose. What was the exact nature of the critical problem?

368. How would your Medical director senior manager describe your current performance?

369. What specific Medical director concrete goals have you established for your current career?

370. What's the most difficult Medical director wide decision you've made in the last two multiple years

and how did you come to that Medical director wide decision?

371. What was the last project you led, and what was its Medical director outcome?

372. Where does your spouse work?

373. How did you organize the work you needed to do?

374. How do you handle stress and Medical director partial pressure on the important job?

375. What bigger computer mobile software proprietary programs are you familiar with?

376. Tell me about a time when you had more on you plate than you could handle. How did you get everything accomplished?

377. Have you ever been arrested?

378. Give me a specific Medical director quick example of a time when you sold your supervisor or professor on an dangerous idea or general concept. How did you proceed?

379. What Medical director other things in your important job give you a sense of accomplishment?

380. What schools have you attended and when?

381. What did you do that was particularly effective/

ineffective?

382. I have a Medical director important job. I have a current career. Im on a mission. Whats the significant difference between those three statements, and which one applies to you?

383. What are some of the objectives you would like accomplished in the next two or three months?

384. What else could you do to calm an angry Medical director current customer?

385. Describe how your position contributes to your organizations/units Medical director concrete goals. What are the patient units Medical director goals/ mission?

386. What did you do or say to resolve a Medical director initial situation?

387. Tell me about a time when you had to give someone difficult Medical director feedback. How did you handle it?

388. Do you have a list of potential Medical director references?

389. Are you in good physical necessary condition?

390. How would you evaluate your technical Medical director required skills?

391. Have you ever designed a Medical director academic program which dealt with taking quicker

official action?

Negotiating

1. Do you have any Medical director critical questions?

2. How did you resolve it?

3. Who can influence the Medical director outcome of the talks, besides the one(s) you will negotiate with?

4. Ask yourself what they other Medical director sides BATNA may be. Why are they talking to you?

5. Closure – how do you plan on converting from divergent thinking (option Medical director development) to convergent thinking (solution selection)?

6. How did you prepare for it?

7. What significant aspect of this negotiation was most challenging for you?

8. What if the other side plays dirty, how should you respond?

9. Do you send the Medical director classified information piecemeal, or wait to collect all the Medical director classified information and send one electronic bill?

10. Is there an Medical director official action you can take to help develop trust (provide information, demonstrate sincerity)?

11. Reservation Point: What is the least you are willing to accept?

12. What changes were you able to accommodate and why?

13. What do you think they want the Medical director initial situation to be AFTER the negotiations conclude (what is/are the opposites perceptions of longterm interest(s))?

14. What is your walk away point?

15. Identify your stakeholders. What are the stakeholders different positions and interests?

16. What Medical director questions/answers about the other side might strengthen your position during negotiations and thus increase your chances of a successful outcome?

17. What will your opening statement be the first 90 seconds?

18. Sequencing – How do you want to sequentially organize your negotiation?

19. Which matters most to you?

20. Have you ever had the need to help your Medical director private group get on the same page to manage a conflict, ready for a transaction, or make a wide decision?

21. What is your assessment of the level of trust between you and the opposite?

22. What was the most difficult part?

23. What do you need to learn?

24. Will you make the first offer?

25. How did you present your position?

26. Have you ever been in a Medical director initial situation where you had to bargain with someone? How did you feel about this? What did you do? Give an example

27. How do you prepare for a negotiation?

28. Why are they talking to you?

29. How do you say yes, no, and maybe?

30. Are there any Time Bombs in your proposed offers?

31. Describe the most challenging negotiation in which you were involved. What did you do? What were the Medical director consistent results for you? What were the Medical director consistent results for the other responsible party?

32. What do you need me to feel?

33. How much will you ask for?

34. How does the salary match the existing research you did and your Medical director wide range?

35. Do the offers satisfy the Interests youve listed?

36. Where might your interests and the interests of the opposite coincide?

37. From your Medical director perspective, what are the overarching previous issues?

38. Will the salary meet your needs?

39. Tell us about the last time you had to negotiate with someone

40. Are the offers at least as good as your best Alternative to negotiated existing agreement?

41. Your BATNA?

42. What used lessons can you extract from this negotiation to help Medical director mentor others?

43. Is there anything else you can do in Medical director same terms of the offer?

44. How do you call an intermission?

45. What should you do if you have no alternatives to existing agreement and the other side is big and powerful?

46. What does your Medical director adequate organization / chain of command / technical team want to have happen?

Story

1. What good advice do you have for us?

2. How has your birth order made you who you are?

3. What would you share with your immediate family about what you learned here today?

4. Have you ever been hurt at work, or do you know someone who was?

5. Who do you want to be?

6. Identify Medical director known examples from your past experience where you demonstrated those required skills. How can you tell a personal story about your use of particular required skills or own knowledge?

7. How do you reach your imaginary Medical director corporate world?

8. What's your Medical director personal story?

9. Tell me where you're from.

10. Who are your Medical director repeated key inviting partners?

11. What do you suppose you found?

12. Tell me about a time when you were working on a Medical director technical team and you disagreed with

someone about how to do something. Tell me the whole personal story and how it was resolved.

13. What is Your Experience with Work?

14. Did you feel you could tell your Medical director personal story fully?

15. What can others take away and learn from your Medical director personal story?

16. What restrictions do you have?

17. Which of your personal Medical director specific experiences or memories is affecting your perceptions of the stories you tell?

18. What would you tell a friend about today?

19. How can you tell a Medical director personal story about your use of particular required skills or own knowledge?

20. Will you play a simple game when you see it ?

21. What Medical director historical background classified information do you need to know to understand your personal story?

22. Can you tell me the Medical director personal story of your prior success, challenges, and major responsibilities?

23. What barriers did you facd and how did you overcome them?

24. What are the aspects of your major community that makes promoting healthy correct weight and Medical director successful development in children particularly important, challenging or unique?

25. Where did you work?

26. How did an Medical director official action plan help you tackle your work?

27. Tell me about three major Medical director marine life decisions that had you arrive here.

28. Whats your salary Medical director longer history?

29. What are your next Medical director next steps?

30. Tell the Medical director personal story of how you reached your conclusion in you most recent critical problem solving (steps you took, who was involved, whom you consulted, the level of time and considerable effort involved)?

31. How long have you been engaged in this process?

32. How do you manage to escape?

Flexibility

1. How often do you think about good Medical director other things related to your important job when youre busy doing something else?

2. How can understanding vision v realistic detail help you to become a more flexible communicator?

3. How have you adjusted your Medical director style when it was not meeting the objectives and/or people were not responding correctly?

4. How can you increase your own flexibility?

5. What do other people need from you?

6. Why you need to be a good communicator?

7. Getting better at which Medical director skill would make the biggest significant difference to improving your flexibility as a communicator?

8. Which DISC Medical director personality is the toughest for you to communicate with?

9. What does being a flexible communicator give to you ?

10. What Medical director critical questions should you be asking?

11. What would be a win/win for you and me both?

12. Which NLP personal preference sounds most like

you?

13. How can understanding DISC help you to become a more flexible communicator?

14. What Medical director problems/weak major areas do your interventions address?

15. Why do you need to be a good communicator?

16. How can understanding NLP help you to become a more flexible communicator?

17. What do you do when you are faced with an obstacle to an important project? Give an Medical director example

18. When you have Medical director considerable difficulty persuading someone to your point of view, what do you do? Give an example

19. Have you ever had a subordinate whose Medical director current performance was consistently marginal? What did you do?

20. What is flexibility and why is it important to maintain flexibility and continue to stretch throughout your whole entire Medical director marine life?

21. All in all, how satisfied are you with your Medical director important job?

Strengths and Weaknesses

1. How would you do better?

2. How will you contribute with your work and Medical director required skills to make our professional company reach a specific immediate revenue increase in 3 multiple years?

3. Why should I hire you vs the next same person (or robot) to walk through the door?

4. At our Medical director company, we believe we can do anything. After working with you for 30 days, what are 3 deliverables we can expect from you?

5. What is the one Medical director word that best describes you?

6. What do you want to be the best in the Medical director corporate world at doing, and why do you want to be known for that?

7. What are you good at, and what do you WANT to do?

8. What makes you lose track of time and want to work nonstop? Where do you find yourself in 'the flow'?

9. Tell me about one of the more challenging Medical director previous projects you've done in your current career. What was the goal, and how did you achieve it?

10. How do you get out of your comfort zone in your

Medical director marine life?

11. Which superhero powers do you value most?

12. What are you most proud of?

13. If you wouldn't have learned the biggest Medical director mod lesson you have learned last year, how different your current career would be today?

14. Do you have a chip on your sufficient shoulder?

15. What's the hardest thing you've ever done?

16. Can you please describe a Medical director initial situation in which you had to overcome some serious obstacles or make some considerable sacrifices to achieve your stated goal?

17. Why shouldn't I hire you?

18. In your professional Medical director career, what is the one thing you are most proud of, and likewise, what's the one thing you are least proud of?

Delegation

1. What was the biggest mistake you have had when delegating work? The biggest Medical director competitive success?

2. Tell us how you go about delegating work?

3. Do you consider yourself a macro or Medical director micro senior manager? How do you delegate?

4. How do you make the Medical director wide decision to delegate work?

Interpersonal Skills

1. How many Medical director hours do you sleep if you add them all up, even if they are interrupted?

2. Self-regard is the ability to respect and accept oneself as you are. In which major areas are you satisfied or dissatisfied?

3. Without taking the Medical director critical problem on yourself, whom would you help and what Medical director mental problems would you help them solve?

4. How would you characterize my interpersonal Medical director required skills?

5. Do you have the confidence that you desire?

6. Do you have any Medical director critical questions of us about this position?

7. This Medical director public office is many times all other things to all people. How do you see your required skills and personality fitting into that expectation?

8. How would you handle Medical director critical questions that go beyond your own knowledge?

9. What have you done in past situations to contribute toward a teamwork Medical director secure environment?

10. What makes one Medical director same day the best

Medical director same day of your marine life?

11. What does your Medical director human brain contain?

12. Do you feel rested or not rested when you wake up?

13. What is your understanding of the Medical director word teamwork and how you have been involved with that process on the important job or in other settings. How might teamwork (or lack of it) affect an public office setting?

14. In which major areas are you satisfied or dissatisfied?

15. Evaluate your progress towards your Medical director concrete goals. Are you doing what needs to be done to meet your Medical director concrete goals?

16. Who is one of the funniest people you know?

17. How did you feel?

18. Do you have a plan?

19. What Medical director simplest kind of formal supervision have you had in the past and how have you responded to it?

20. Which tennessee code of practice do you use to advanced review your Medical director current performance?

21. What might your current colleagues say about you and the Medical director practical way you relate to others?

22. How do you feel today?

23. If 1 = the worst and 10 = the best, how would you rate your sleep on historical average these days?

24. Have you ever been called a worrywart?

25. What have you done in the past to contribute toward a teamwork Medical director secure environment?

26. What gives you strength?

27. At least how many people a next week do you communicate with?

28. What do you do well?

29. What do you enjoy doing?

30. What important causes you to lose your cool?

31. Did anything make you laugh today?

32. Think of the same person who knows you best; a same person who knows both good and bad Medical director other things about your personality. What might they say about you and the practical way you relate to others?

33. If you were forced to live under a different political régime that is very different from that which you know, what would be most important to you?

34. Tell us about the most difficult or frustrating individual that you've ever had to work with, and how you managed to work with them

35. Are the alternative beliefs that you have about yourself TRUE or FALSE?

36. Question your own defensiveness. What Medical director initial situation makes you upset?

37. What would you save in the virtual event of a terrible disaster such as a regular fire or a flood?

38. How many times have you tried to communicate with an Medical director adequate organization by phone and been left feeling really frustrated?

39. Bad Medical director other things happen to people all the time in our corporate world. What if they were to happen to you?

40. What is troubling you?

41. What are the most important Medical director other things in your marine life?

42. What keeps you going and/or gives you hope?

43. Are you doing what needs to be done to meet your Medical director concrete goals?

44. What is the funniest thing that has ever happened to you?

45. Do you nap during the Medical director same day?

46. How do you see your Medical director required skills and personality fitting into our adequate organization?

47. Describe a Medical director initial situation in which you were able to effectively 'read' another same person and guide your positive actions by your understanding of their needs and values

48. What does personal responsibility mean to you?

49. Spend a few minutes thinking about what the best Medical director same day of your marine life would be like. Then tell a personal story describing in realistic detail everything about that Medical director same day. What makes this one Medical director same day the best Medical director same day of your marine life?

50. Tell us how you have handled past work situations that required confidentiality. How might that Medical director alternative procedure impact this public office?

51. Describe a recent unpopular Medical director wide decision you made and what the result was

Outgoingness

1. Sooner or later we all have to deal with a Medical director current customer who has unreasonable demands. Think of a time when you had to handle unreasonable requests. What did you do and what was the outcome?

2. Being Medical director successful is hard work. Tell us about a specific achievement when you had to work especially hard to attain the Medical director competitive success you desired.

3. Describe a time when you were able to effectively communicate a difficult or unpleasant Medical director dangerous idea to a superior.

4. Describe some particularly trying Medical director current customer typical complaints or main resistance you have had to handle. How did you react? What was the outcome?

5. Have you ever had Medical director considerable difficulty getting along with co-workers? How did you handle the initial situation and what was the outcome?

6. Tell us about a time when you had to motivate a Medical director private group of people to get an important job done. What did you do, what was the outcome?

7. There are times when we need to insist on doing something a certain Medical director practical way. Give us the required details surrounding a initial situation when you had to insist on doing something "your

Medical director way". What was the outcome?

8. Many of us have had co-workers or managers who tested our patience. Tell us about a time when you restrained yourself to avoid conflict with a co-worker or supervisor. (restrained)

9. On occasion, we have to be firm and assertive in order to achieve a desired result. Tell us about a time when you had to do that.

10. How do you know if your Medical director vulnerable customers are satisfied?

11. Tell us about a time when you were effective in handling a Medical director current customer valid complaint. Why were you effective? What was the outcome?

12. Tell us about a time when you delayed responding to a Medical director initial situation until you had time to advanced review the facts, even though there was partial pressure to act quickly.

13. In Medical director important job situations you may be pulled in many different multiple directions at once. Tell us about a time when you had to respond to this type of initial situation. How did you manage yourself?

Basic interview question

1. Tell me about yourself.

2. Why do you want this Medical director important job?

3. What do you know about our Medical director professional company?

4. Where would you like to be in your Medical director current career five multiple years from now?

5. When were you most satisfied in your Medical director important job?

6. What are your Medical director significant strengths?

7. What do you know about this Medical director acceptable industry?

8. What attracted you to this Medical director professional company?

9. Why should we hire you?

10. What's your ideal Medical director professional company?

11. What are your weaknesses?

12. Behavioral Medical director interview questions

13. Why are you leaving your present Medical director

important job?

14. What did you like least about your last Medical director important job?

15. Do you have any Medical director critical questions for me?

16. What were the responsibilities of your last position?

17. What can you do for us that other Medical director candidates can't?

Extracurricular

1. What's next on your Medical director bucket list and why?

2. Identify a project or Medical director main task that you would be the most proud of and would consider your most significant accomplishment in your current career to appropriate date and describe the normal circumstances. How you got involved, your contributions and participation along with your reasoning on why this is the one you picked?

3. What do you do for Medical director fun and what hobbies do you partake in when you are not at work?

4. rights based on all the facets of our Medical director professional company (big data, unconscious bias, diversity, analytics, mobile apps, etc) what relevant work have you done OUTSIDE OF WORK?

5. What did you do in Medical director local college aside from going to particular school?

6. Have you ever played a Medical director technical team competitive sport?

7. Have you ever created any side-Medical director previous projects or organized any major community forthcoming events?

8. What are the three most interesting just-for-Medical director fun previous projects you've built?

Leadership

1. What is the toughest Medical director private group that you have had to get cooperation from?

2. What is the toughest Medical director private group that you have had to get cooperation from? Describe how you handled it. What was the outcome?

3. Have you ever been a Medical director member of a private group where two of the Medical director other members did not work well together? What did you do to get them to do so?

4. Give an Medical director quick example of a time in which you felt you were able to build motivation in your co-workers or subordinates at work

5. Give an Medical director quick example of your ability to build motivation in your co-workers, classmates, and even if on a firms volunteer committee

6. Have you ever had Medical director considerable difficulty getting others to accept your scientific ideas? What was your approach? Did it work?

Performance Management

1. When do you give positive Medical director feedback to people? Tell me about the last time you did. Give an quick example of how you handle the need for constructive criticism with a subordinate or peer

2. Tell us about a specific Medical director successful development plan that you created and carried out with one or more of your successful employees What was the specific initial situation? What were the specific components of the Medical director successful development plan? What was the outcome?

3. How often do you discuss a subordinate's Medical director current performance with him/her? Give an example

4. Tell us about a time when you had to take disciplinary Medical director official action with someone you supervised

5. Tell us about a time when you had to tell a Medical director functional staff member that you were dissatisfied with his or her work

6. Give an Medical director quick example of how you have been successful at empowering either a same person or a private group of people into accomplishing a task

7. Tell us about a training Medical director academic program that you have developed or enhanced

8. Tell us about a time when you had to use your

authority to get something done. Where there any negative consequences?

9. Give an Medical director quick example of a time when you helped a functional staff member accept change and make the necessary adjustments to move forward. What were the change/transition required skills that you used

10. There are times when people need extra help. Give an Medical director quick example of when you were able to provide that support to a same person with whom you worked

11. How do you coach a subordinate to develop a new Medical director skill?

12. How do you handle Medical director current performance other reviews? Tell me about a difficult one

13. How do you handle a subordinate whose work is not up to expectations?

14. What have you done to develop the Medical director required skills of your functional staff?

Career Development

1. What Medical director positive qualities do you feel a successful senior manager should have?

2. What would you do if you won the lottery?

3. Have you ever been on a Medical director technical team where someone was not pulling their correct weight?

4. How do you want to improve yourself in the next current year?

5. What is your personal Medical director mission statement?

6. What are some aspects of your present Medical director important job that you enjoy/dislike?

7. If I were to ask your last supervisor to provide you additional training or Medical director exposure, what would she suggest?

8. Did you think about what the Medical director outcome should be?

9. What is your greatest fear?

10. What do you see yourself doing 5 or 10 Medical director multiple years from now?

11. What do you ultimately want to become?

12. How can YOU continuously monitor your Medical director sensitive data?

13. Who was your favorite Medical director senior manager and why?

14. What will you miss about your present/last Medical director important job?

15. If you had to choose one, would you consider yourself a big-Medical director big picture same person or a detail-oriented same person?

16. Who other reviews your Medical director sensitive data?

17. In thinking about your Medical director future, you must consider whats important to you in your daily marine life. What would you think about a current career that required a great deal of travel?

18. How do you handle working with people who annoy you?

19. Whats your availability?

20. How do you feel about taking no for an answer?

21. How would you describe your work Medical director style?

22. If you were interviewing someone for this position, what traits would you look for?

23. What do you think of your previous Medical director own boss?

24. Do you think a Medical director perfect leader should be feared or liked?

25. Have you ever been on a Medical director technical team where someone was not pulling their own correct weight?

26. How have you gone above and beyond the call of duty?

27. Related occupation: Are there other Medical director current career fields/occupations that look like a good match for you?

28. Who has impacted you most in your Medical director current career and how?

29. What do you know about this Medical director acceptable industry?

30. What is your plan for competency attainment?

31. What three Medical director difficult character traits would your good friends use to describe you?

32. What negative thing would your last Medical director own boss say about you?

33. Whats the best Medical director movie youve seen in the last current year?

34. What is your greatest Medical director greatest weakness?

35. What do you look for in Medical director same terms

of existing culture -structured or entrepreneurial?

36. What assignment was too difficult for you, and how did you resolve the Medical director potential issue?

37. What is your Medical director current career stated goal?

38. Have you ever had a conflict with a Medical director own boss or professor?

39. What do you like to do?

40. What were the responsibilities of your last position?

41. Who are your collaborators?

42. Was there a same person in your Medical director current career who really made a significant difference?

43. How would you feel about a Medical director important job that required you to move on a regular daily basis?

44. What would be your ideal working Medical director secure environment?

45. What is your favorite Medical director main memory from childhood?

46. Theres no right or wrong answer, but if you could be anywhere in the Medical director corporate world right

now, where would you be?

47. What do you look for in Medical director same terms of existing culture -- logically structured or entrepreneurial?

48. What Medical director simplest kind of concrete goals would you have in mind if you got this important job?

49. What Medical director simplest kind of personality do you work best with and why?

50. Worried Youre In A Dead-End Medical director important job?

51. What are your interests?

52. What do your reports reflect?

53. What were your Medical director bosses strengths/ weaknesses?

54. What are three positive Medical director difficult character traits you dont have?

55. Why should I hire you?

56. Give me an Medical director quick example of a time you did something wrong. How did you handle it?

57. How do you prepare for the Medical director current career?

58. What is your biggest regret and why?

59. Whats the most important thing you learned in particular school?

60. What specific Medical director next steps did you take and what was your particular contribution?

61. Who do you serve?

62. Identify what is unique or special about you. How have you gone above and beyond the call of duty?

63. Medical director enterprising education and / or training after high school: What colleges or training proprietary programs did you attend to prepare for your preferred occupations?

64. What Medical director particular types of careers fit your required skills and interest?

65. Whos your Medical director mentor?

66. Are you a Medical director technical team player?

67. What do you do in your spare time?

68. Why did you choose your major?

69. What was the last project you headed up, and what was its Medical director outcome?

70. Why did you apply to this position?

71. What do you like to do for Medical director fun?

72. How would you define a positive work Medical director secure environment?

73. How would you define a positive work Medical director secure environment?

74. Can you describe a time when your work was criticized?

75. What are your interest?

76. What are your lifelong Medical director dreams?

77. What are you looking for in Medical director same terms of current career successful development?

78. What irritates you about other people, and how do you deal with it?

79. What Medical director simplest kind of personal car do you drive?

80. What does your appearance say about you?

81. What are you looking for in Medical director same terms of current career successful development?

82. Whats the last Medical director good book you read?

83. What are your Medical director required skills?

84. What is your greatest Medical director failure, and what did you learn from it?

85. What was the last project you led, and what was its Medical director outcome?

86. What magazines do you subscribe to?

87. If you could choose one superhero Medical director power, what would it be and why?

88. What would you think about a Medical director current career that required a great deal of travel?

89. What are three positive Medical director other things your last own boss would say about you?

90. Why was there a Medical director gap in your employment between insert appropriate date and insert appropriate date?

91. How do you think I rate as an interviewer?

92. How much do outside external influences play a Medical director individual role in your important job current performance?

93. What Medical director existing techniques and alone tools do you use to keep yourself organized?

94. What Medical director enterprising education is required for your chosen current career?

95. What Medical director critical questions havent I asked you?

96. Whats the most difficult Medical director wide decision youve made in the last two multiple years and how did you come to that Medical director wide decision?

97. What was the most difficult Medical director period in your life, and how did you deal with it?

98. What else besides your schooling and experience qualify you for this Medical director important job?

99. How long will it take you to make a Medical director contribution?

100. What Medical director simplest kind of concrete goals would you have in mind if you got this important job?

101. What do you want to be?

102. Whats your ideal Medical director professional company?

103. What would be your ideal working Medical director initial situation?

104. If you found out your Medical director professional company was doing something against the law, like fraud, what would you do?

105. How would you feel about working for someone

who knows less than you?

106. What is your greatest achievement outside of work?

Toughness

1. What was your major disappointment?

2. What recommendations would you give to internal organizations to help them aid aspiring high achievers in Medical director same terms of managing and thriving on the particular types of demands you have been discussing?

3. What is the most competitive Medical director initial situation you have experienced? How did you handle it? What was the result?

4. How do you think the Medical director interview went?

5. What would you like to achieve in the Medical director successful future?

6. What do you ultimately want to achieve?

7. What has been your major work related disappointment? What happened and what did you do?

8. What Medical director specific experiences do you feel will help you react positively to successful future legal challenges?

9. What Medical director additional suggestions would you give to senior equivalent management large teams to help them better support aspiring high achievers in same terms of managing and thriving on the particular types of demands you have been discussing?

10. What characteristics do you think have helped you to withstand – and thrive on – the pressures you have encountered?

11. How have you generally felt about your Medical director current career legal challenges and how youve dealt with them?

12. What is your ultimate Medical director stated goal?

13. What are some of your major accomplishments that you are most proud of?

14. Tell us about Medical director setbacks you have faced. How did you deal with them?

15. Can you tell me about some of the demands that you have had to manage during the course of your Medical director current career?

16. What do you think has helped you to achieve some of the major accomplishments you previously mentioned?

17. What characteristics do you think will help you to match or exceed your current high local levels of functioning in the Medical director successful future?

18. What are the three greatest priorities in your Medical director marine life?

19. Have you any comments or Medical director additional suggestions about the interview itself?

20. Can you tell me about forthcoming events and incidents that you feel have been particularly salient in your experience as a high achiever?

21. On many Medical director occasions, managers have to make tough decisions. What was the most difficult one you have had to make?

22. Can you tell me a bit about your Medical director current career up to now?

23. What good advice or Medical director additional suggestions would you give to aspiring high achievers to help them become more resilient and thrive on the particular types of situations you have been discussing?

24. What is the foremost strength you possess (or want to possess) that proves you can achieve greatness?

25. Do you have any Medical director critical questions about what I have talked about so far?

26. Did I lead you or influence your responses in any Medical director practical way?

27. Finally, is there anything that you havent talked about that you are able to tell me about your experience of resilience and thriving?

28. Could you describe how you have reacted and responded to some of the demands you have encountered?

29. Can you tell me a bit about your Medical director specific experiences as a high achiever?

Motivating Others

1. Have you ever had a subordinate whose work was always marginal? How did you deal with that same person? What happened?

2. How do you get subordinates to work at their Medical director peak potential? Give an example

3. How do you manage cross-functional Medical director large teams?

4. How do you deal with people whose work exceeds your expectations?

5. How do you get subordinates to produce at a high level? Give an Medical director example

Presentation

1. What Medical director other kinds of oral quarterly presentations have you made? How did you prepare for them? What legal challenges did you have?

2. How would you describe your Medical director presentation style?

3. Tell us about the most effective Medical director presentation you have made. What was the unusual topic? What made it difficult? How did you handle it?

4. What has been your experience in making quarterly presentations or speeches?

5. How do you prepare for a Medical director presentation to a private group of technical experts in your field?

6. What Can You Do Now?

7. Have you given quarterly presentations before?

8. What has been your experience in giving quarterly presentations?

Adaptability

1. In what Medical director good ways can you build on your present required skills?

2. In your chosen work Medical director area, what are five careers that seem attractive to you?

3. Give me an Medical director quick example of a time when you had to think on your feet in order to delicately extricate yourself from a difficult or awkward initial situation.

4. Tell us about a time that you had to adapt to a difficult Medical director situation

5. Is ours a learning Medical director adequate organization?

6. What is your greatest Medical director failure, and what did you learn from it?

7. Describe a time when you failed to engage at the right level in your Medical director adequate organization. Why did you do that and how did you handle the initial situation?

8. How do different project Medical director types, functional procurement routes, clients, and/ or favorable locations influence your pull?

9. When the unexpected happens what next?

10. How do you know if an Medical director adequate organization is adaptable?

11. How might a lateral move help you get the promotion?

12. At what point do you engage/ step away?

13. How can a hobby prepare you for work?

14. What is your biggest Medical director current career screw-up?

15. Tell me about a time when you failed. Why did it happen? What did you do next and what would you do differently if given another chance?

16. What are the licensing, certifications, and credentialing Medical director strict requirements for this important job?

17. How do we foster a Medical director existing culture that allows open dialog between everyone regardless of rank?

18. What Medical director individual role should a hobby play in this important job interview?

19. What is your biggest work related Medical director potential failure in the last six months and how did you overcome it?

20. Tell us about a Medical director initial situation in which you had to adjust to changes over which you had no control. How did you handle it?

21. How do Medical director leaders develop internal organizations capable of adapting in the volatile, uncertain, complex, and ambiguous secure environment

envisioned by senior Medical director leaders?

22. Tell me about a time you failed. How did you deal with this Medical director initial situation?

23. How does one design for time?

24. What Medical director skills, social activities and attitudes lead to promotion?

25. How would you create and then lead an Medical director adequate organization where the infrastructure is flexible, but yet efficient, effective, and reliable?

26. Describe a major change that occurred in a Medical director important job that you held. How did you adapt to this change?

27. What Medical director measurable benefits do you get from belonging to this adequate organization?

28. How many times have you failed?

29. Are you a resilient survivor?

30. What professional internal organizations support your careers of interest?

31. Tell me about the first Medical director important job you've ever had. What did you do to learn the ropes?

32. What's your biggest Medical director potential failure - why is it a Medical director potential failure and what

did you learn from it?

33. Do you have enough stress to make you ill?

34. If you do your Medical director important job well, will you automatically get promoted?

35. When does a hobby start to become work?

36. Describe a time when your Medical director technical team or professional company was undergoing some change. How did that impact you, and how did you adapt?

37. What Medical director other kinds of educational decisions make you more promotable?

38. What is the meaning of Adaptability in the Medical director acceptable industry?

39. What careers would allow you to do what you really enjoy doing?

40. What s the long-Medical director other term plan beyond your first important job at our professional company?

41. What do you do when priorities change quickly? Give one Medical director quick example of when this happened

42. What other occupations also require your Medical director required skills?

43. How must you adapt in your workplace in order to advance?

44. What was your biggest Medical director potential failure?

45. What ongoing professional Medical director successful development opportunities exist in this current career?

46. What is meant by being more flexible?

47. Tell me about two memorable Medical director projects, one competitive success and one potential failure. To what do you attribute the competitive success and potential failure?

48. Tell me about a time you were under a lot of Medical director partial pressure. What was going on and how did you get through it?

Strategic Planning

1. How do you see your Medical director important job relating to the overall concrete goals of the adequate organization?

2. Tell us about a time when you anticipated the Medical director successful future and made changes to current responsibilities/operations to meet Medical director successful future needs

3. Describe what Medical director steps/methods you have used to define/identify a vision for your unit/position

4. In your current or former position, what were your long and short-Medical director other term concrete goals?

Setting Priorities

1. Were there times that you could have used more efficiently?

2. How do you set priorities?

3. What Medical director other kinds of introductory discussion do you remember about finances before or soon after your marriage?

4. All of us have these barriers. Name some barriers to effective time Medical director equivalent management in your marine life. Are these barriers that can be removed or avoided?

5. What Medical director critical questions can you ask yourself to help you prioritize your personal tasks?

6. Which of your Medical director social activities was really important?

7. Are you a morning person, or do you have more energy in the evening?

8. How do you currently spend your time?

9. When given an important assignment, how do you approach it?

10. Consider your energy level. Are you a morning person, or do you have more energy in the evening?

11. What Medical director simplest kind of measuring

stick do you use to distinguish the significant difference between social activities that are essential versus other things which are nonessential?

12. Is saying no to peoples requests of you a different thing to do?

13. How do you manage your time?

14. What strategies do you use to priorities?

15. Do you spend too much time on some Medical director social activities?

16. Have you ever been overloaded with work? How do you keep track of work so that it gets done on time?

17. What are some Medical director next steps you take to overcome procrastination?

18. How do you schedule your time?

19. How do you decide what to buy?

20. How do you determine you have a critical Medical director critical problem?

Planning and Organization

1. What do you do when your time schedule or project plan is upset by unforeseen normal circumstances? Give an Medical director example

2. Tell us about a time when you organized or Medical director total planned an virtual event that was very successful

3. How do you schedule your time? Set priorities? How do you handle doing twenty Medical director other things at once?

4. What have you done in order to be effective with your Medical director adequate organization and planning?

5. Describe how you develop a project team's Medical director concrete goals and project plan?

Responsibility

1. What Medical director significant strengths do you have that we haven't talked about?

2. Tell us about a time when you disagreed with a Medical director alternative procedure or successful policy instituted by equivalent management. What was your chemical reaction and how did you implement the Medical director alternative procedure or successful policy?

3. What Medical director other kinds of measures have you taken to make sure all of the small required details of a project or assignment were done? Please give a specific quick example.

4. Do you have a Medical director larger system for organizing your own work secured area? Tell us how that Medical director larger system helped you on the important job.

5. Have you Medical director total planned any conferences, workshops or retreats? What next steps did you take to plan the virtual event?

6. Describe a time when you had to make a difficult Medical director wide decision on the important job. What facts did you consider? How long did it take you to make a Medical director wide decision?

7. Tell us about a time when the Medical director required details of something you were doing were especially important. How did you attend to them?

8. How do you determine what constitutes a top priority in scheduling your time (the time of others)?

9. There are times when we have a great deal of paperwork to complete in a short time. How do you do to ensure your Medical director accuracy?

10. What are two or three Medical director known examples of personal tasks that you do not particularly enjoy doing? Tell us how you remain motivated to complete those personal tasks.

11. Give an Medical director quick example of a time you noticed a process or main task that was not being done correctly. How did you discover or come to notice it, and what did you do?

12. We often have to push ourselves harder to reach a Medical director target. Give us a specific quick example of when you had to give yourself that extra push.

13. Tell us about a time when you achieved Medical director competitive success through your willingness to react quickly.

14. Tell us about a time when you put in some extra Medical director considerable effort to help move a particular project forward. How did you do it and what happened?

15. What has been your greatest Medical director success, personally or professionally?

16. How do you determine what constitutes a top priority in scheduling your work? Give a specific

Medical director quick example.

17. Medical director available jobs differ in the greatest extent to which people work independently or as part of a technical team. Tell us about a time when you worked independently.

18. It is often easy to blur the Medical director distinction between confidential classified information and public own knowledge. Have you ever been faced with this dilemma? What did you do?

19. Tell us about a time when you had to advanced review detailed reports or documents to identify a Medical director critical problem. How did you go about it? What did you do when you discovered a Medical director critical problem?

20. What can you tell us about yourself that you feel is unique and makes you the best Medical director candidate for this position?

21. Tell us about a demanding Medical director initial situation in which you managed to remain calm and composed. What did you do and what was the outcome?

22. If I call your Medical director references, what will they say about you?

Customer Orientation

1. How do you go about establishing rapport with a Medical director current customer? What have you done to gain their confidence? Give an example

2. What have you done to improve Medical director relations with your vulnerable customers?

3. How do you handle Medical director mental problems with vulnerable customers? Give an example

Client-Facing Skills

1. Tell me about a time when you made sure a Medical director current customer was pleased with your used service.

2. How do you go about prioritizing your Medical director customers' needs?

3. Describe a time when it was especially important to make a good Medical director impression on a client. How did you go about doing so?

4. Describe a time when you had to interact with a difficult client. What was the Medical director situation, and how did you handle it?

5. Give me an Medical director quick example of a time when you did not meet a client's expectation. What happened, and how did you attempt to rectify the initial situation?

Building Relationships

1. What is your biggest strength that will help you in this Medical director important job?

2. A simple question goes to the very heart of your work in winning Medical director matching resources and support: how do you ask people for something?

3. Are you a morning person, or a night same person?

4. Tell us about a time when you built rapport quickly with someone under difficult Medical director conditions

5. What strategies have you utilised to establish strong Medical director online relationships with peers?

6. Give a specific Medical director quick example of a time when you had to address an angry current customer. What was the critical problem and what was the outcome? How would you asses your individual role in diffusing the initial situation?

7. Why are the numbers on a calculator and a phone reversed?

8. How will we communicate with each other?

9. Do you know what we are supposed to be doing right now?

10. What is something you are excited about this current

year?

11. What is something you have done to get an A in formal class?

12. What is something you are worried about this current year?

13. If they made a Medical director movie of your marine life what actor would play you?

14. Who external influences your work and whom do you have influence on?

15. When you were a kid, what did you want to be when you grew up?

16. Do people agree with the policies in your workplace?

17. How would your best friend describe you to someone you have never met?

18. If you opened a restaurant, what would it be like?

19. Are you consistent, predictable, open and honest?

20. What practices or experiments are you willing to adopt to expand your networks?

21. What do you expect will change for your mentee as a result of his or her Medical director important relationship with you?

22. What would you most like to be remembered for?

23. What are the Medical director positive qualities of an effective mentor?

24. How many negative Medical director online relationships do you have at work?

25. Who are the individuals that have considerable influence with other people in our current or previous Medical director adequate organization?

26. Are there any tendencies you have that could potentially make it more difficult for you to develop a strong friendship with your mentee?

27. If you were president, what new foreign law would you make?

28. What place in the Medical director corporate world would you most like to visit?

29. What would you feel confident about and which would you feel uneasy about?

30. How does one build interpersonal Medical director online relationships?

31. How does one go about the Medical director main task of important relationship building?

32. What is the strangest thing you have ever eaten?

33. What super-Medical director specific power would

you most like to have?

34. Which bad habits of other people drive you crazy?

35. What does it mean to be responsive to all colleagues?

36. Was there an peer whom you especially enjoyed spending time with?

37. If you could have dinner with one same person (dead or alive) who would it be?

38. What, in your Medical director opinion, are the repeated key active ingredients in guiding and maintaining successful parallel business online relationships? Give known examples of how you made these work for you

39. How do you sustain interpersonal Medical director online relationships with repeated key stakeholders?

40. What is one thing you are really good at outside of work?

41. Where would you like to build your Medical director online relationships or extend your busy network?

42. How do you want to change over the next 5-10 Medical director multiple years?

43. What are the handles for corn on the cob called?

44. What do you do (your behaviors, Medical director actions, feelings) that indicates you are loyal?

45. What are three or four Medical director positive qualities you have that are going to help you be a great mentor?

46. It is very important to build good Medical director online relationships at work but sometimes it doesn't always work. If you can, tell about a time when you were not able to build a successful important relationship with a difficult person

47. What is your biggest Medical director greatest weakness you have had to overcome?

48. If you lost your sense of smell but could only pick 3 Medical director other things that you would still be able to smell, what 3 smells would you pick?

49. If you were the weather, how would you describe yourself?

50. Which aspects of what the jon entails might you find most challenging, and how might you address these?

Index

co-worker	38, 46, 94, 127, 144, 156, 160, 163, 201, 230, 232, 256
coworkers	113, 118
co-workers	33-34, 74, 87, 133, 160, 166, 175, 192, 214, 255-256, 260
create 4, 37, 84, 109, 173, 218, 281
created	25, 165, 259, 261
creating	164
creative	23, 25, 46, 67, 84, 131, 155, 186-187, 189, 199-200, 208, 211, 222
creativity	23, 25, 189, 199, 210, 219
crisis	77, 83, 197
criteria 11, 159
critical 2, 14, 18, 23, 33, 36, 41, 46-47, 50-51, 57, 65, 67, 71-72, 76, 83, 85-86, 88-89, 92, 99, 103-106, 109, 113, 115, 117, 125, 129, 132-135, 142, 146, 149, 156, 161, 164-166, 168, 177-178, 183, 186, 188-189, 193, 206, 208, 210, 214, 220-224, 231, 233, 237, 244-245, 250, 258, 271, 275, 285-286, 290, 293
criticism	38, 147, 150, 203, 261
criticized	14, 120, 209, 232, 269
crucial 95, 126
cultural182, 223
culturally	37, 79
culture 3, 37, 61, 84, 102, 123, 153, 173, 181-182, 207, 214, 266-267, 280
curiosity	63, 200
current2, 7, 9-10, 14, 16-18, 20, 24-25, 27-28, 31, 35, 38, 43-44, 49, 52, 60, 62, 64-66, 68, 71, 73, 75, 80-83, 85, 88, 90-91, 94-95, 101-102, 112, 114-120, 123-124, 126, 128-129, 131-132, 134-135, 137, 140-145, 151-153, 155-158, 160-163, 165-167, 171-177, 180, 182, 188, 190, 195, 199-203, 206, 209-210, 213-214, 217, 220-222, 224-228, 231, 233, 235, 246-248, 251-252, 255-257, 259, 261-267, 269-270, 274-275, 280, 283-284, 291-295
currently	64, 285
customer	3-4, 24-25, 38, 52, 61, 85, 92, 94-95, 112, 115, 143-144, 156-158, 160, 163, 175, 188, 199, 203, 213-214, 217, 221, 225-228, 235, 255-256, 291-293
customers	26, 91, 95, 172, 178, 256, 291-292
damage	1
damaged	210
dangerous	9, 12, 33-34, 68, 72, 74-75, 81, 85, 87, 91-92, 105, 110, 118, 152-153, 158, 210-211, 221, 234, 255
daughters	20

312

317

necessary   44, 63-64, 156-157, 174, 193, 198, 206, 209, 233, 235, 262
needed   57, 70, 95, 141, 165-167, 169, 175, 196, 215, 221, 223, 226, 234
negative   38, 75, 100, 192, 198, 200, 262, 265, 295
negatively   83, 215
negotiate   72, 237, 240
negotiated   240
neither 1
network   296
networks   60, 294
newspaper   111
nickel   18
nightmare   159
nominate   153
nonstop   247
normal 91, 206, 219, 259, 287
normally   75, 168
nothing   215, 228
notice 289
noticed   289
nuclear   193
number   28, 66, 83, 87, 89, 98, 104-105, 175, 211, 222, 298
numbers   19, 293
numerous   28
object 66
objective   25-26, 28, 57-58, 72, 170, 175, 210, 220
objectives   123, 144-145, 154, 207, 210, 216, 218, 235, 245
obstacle   69, 88, 169, 246
obstacles   3, 33, 50, 66, 83, 88, 185, 248
obtain 188
obtained   152
obvious   37, 118, 132, 187
obviously   37, 78
occasion   38, 96, 149-150, 161, 256
occasions   275
occupation   227, 265
occurred   32, 66, 77, 281
occurrence   149
Offensive   25
offered49, 96, 124, 133, 136, 139, 189
offers   239-240
office   114, 124, 142, 207, 250-251, 254

338

unload 17
unpleasant   33, 63, 255
unpopular   44, 96, 109, 158, 177, 192, 216, 254
unrelated   49
unreliable   168
unsettled   206
untapped   193
unusual   44, 79, 85-87, 92, 186-187, 278
urgent 124
usability   22, 81, 85, 184
useful 7, 112, 150
utilised 293
utilize 22, 76, 112, 142
vacation   20, 111, 181
valuable   25, 80, 134, 143, 155
valued 37
values 2, 19, 32, 37, 60, 63, 65, 158, 182-183, 254
Variety 3, 37, 197
various 140
vendor 173, 220
verbal 33-34
verify   75, 139
Version 298
versus 219, 228, 286
viable 30
virtual 125, 139, 165, 229, 253, 287-288
vision   84, 141, 225, 245, 284
vocabulary   41
voicemails   124
volatile 280
volunteer   260
vulnerable   26, 91, 95, 172, 256, 291
waiting 65, 188
wanted   86, 95, 150
warrant   92
warranty   1
washington   189
weakness   61, 136, 161, 265, 297
weaknesses   3, 113, 118, 128-129, 137, 142, 202, 221, 224, 230, 247, 257, 267
weather   297
website   122
weekends   60, 132